Date Du

A|

Transformations
in French Business

Recent Titles from Quorum Books

Transformations
in French Business

POLITICAL, ECONOMIC, AND CULTURAL CHANGES FROM 1981 TO 1987

Edited by
Judith Frommer & Janice McCormick

Foreword by Jacques Maisonrouge

Q

QUORUM BOOKS
NEW YORK • WESTPORT, CONNECTICUT • LONDON

Library of Congress Cataloging-in-Publication Data

Transformations in French business : political, economic, and cultural
  changes from 1981 to 1987 / edited by Judith Frommer and Janice
  McCormick ; foreword by Jacques Maisonrouge.
    p.   cm.
    Includes index.
    ISBN 0–89930–387–0 (lib. bdg. : alk. paper)
    1. Industry and state—France. 2. France—Economic policy—1981–
3. France—Politics and government—1981– 4. France—Commerce.
I. Frommer, Judith. II. McCormick, Janice. III. Maisonrouge,
Jacques, 1924–   .
HD3616.F82T73   1989
338.944—dc19   88–18506

British Library Cataloguing in Publication Data is available.

Library of Congress Catalog Card Number: 88–18506
ISBN: 0–89930–387–0

First published in 1989 by Quorum Books

Greenwood Press, Inc.
88 Post Road West, Westport, Connecticut   06881

Printed in the United States of America

The paper used in this book complies with the
Permanent Paper Standard issued by the National
Information Standards Organization (Z39.48–1984).

10   9   8   7   6   5   4   3   2   1

Contents

Foreword

Jacques Maisonrouge

As Americans and French begin preparations to celebrate the two-hundredth anniversary of the French Revolution in 1989, they will undoubtedly think about the great movement of ideas that arose in the eighteenth century: human rights and culture. This cooperation will recall the friendship between the two countries, born from wars fought together and common goals for the defense of freedom.

These memories and good feelings based on history, while appreciated by the French, are in contrast with current American impressions of France. Unfortunately, most Americans have an image of France that does not correspond to present-day French realities. For example, how many Americans would believe that, not long ago, I attended a meeting of the heads of 150 French companies considered "world leaders" in their own fields? I am sure that if an opinion poll were conducted in the United States asking Americans how many French companies they thought were world leaders in their fields, the answer would be no more than ten or fifteen. Consequently, it is time to set the record straight. *Transformations in French Business* is such an attempt.

The traditional image of French is positive, and this is not only the result of advertising and public relations. Americans have always recognized France's strength in the areas of fashion, wines, spirits, mineral waters, culture, agrobusiness, and tourism, and they have accepted that we have a high quality of life. We French must ensure that these strong points remain strong, that the products and services offered are of high quality, and that they continue to be known. As proof that the French government is behind such an effort, the Ministry of Tourism launched a remarkable campaign this year to encourage the French to give a better welcome to visitors to our country.

On the other hand, it is not well perceived that France has, in the last thirty years, become a major scientific and industrial country, capable of competing with the Germans, British, Italians, Americans, and even the Japanese, with regard to sophisticated products. France has become not only the fourth-largest industrial country in the free world, but also the fourth-largest exporter. France's share of world exports grew from 5.9 percent in 1986 to 6.1 percent in 1987, the highest percentage since 1972.

What do we export? To most countries we export high technology or "medium" technology products, such as helicopters, airplanes, fissile materials, chemical products, special steels, computers, software, and pharmaceuticals. A tendency toward a higher proportion of manufactured goods in our exports, now about 80 percent, has been accelerated by legislative changes introduced by the Fabius government and pushed by the Chirac government.

The most important factor in our improving business picture is, perhaps, the decreasing influence of outdated ideologies like Marxism. The French now like business and understand what it takes to be successful in world markets. Although there are still some who consider that all efforts should be directed toward Europe, most younger people and a few knowledgeable older ones now recognize the global character of today's markets and the absurdity of replacing an obsolete nationalism with a Europeanism that would itself become rapidly obsolete. While it is true that Europe as a whole is the largest market in the world, we must not forget that North America is second and Japan third.

My growing optimism about France's place in the world economy is the result of significant changes in attitude and legislation that have occurred in France in the past two years. First, the French have begun to show a definite willingness to discover their weak points. An example of this new approach is the recognition that research and development (R&D) expenditures have been insufficient. During 1987, the Ministry of Industry launched a major effort to convince French companies to invest more in R&D and, in general, in innovation. In fact, R&D is only 1.3 percent of the gross national product (GNP) in France, while it is 1.7 percent to 1.8 percent of GNP in Germany, Japan, and the United States. In an effort to remedy this situation, the government has recently instituted fiscal reforms, such as tax credits for R&D, and educational measures that include funds to transfer engineers and scientists from national laboratories and universities to the private sector, incentives to increase the number of R&D contracts between universities and companies, and the creation of new technical institutions. There has also been increased investment in the training of scientists, engineers, and marketing and management experts. New postgraduate education facilities are flourishing. If it is true that understanding a problem is a giant step toward solving it, then the French, who have finally begun to understand the importance of R&D, are well on the way to improving their situation in this area.

Another example of the new French willingness to recognize weaknesses concerns marketing. Many French companies have been unable to sell well in foreign countries because they are prisoners of the past. These companies are more comfortable doing business with French-speaking countries in Europe and

Africa, though Germany is France's most important commercial partner. Young people, however, are realizing the importance of learning English, and even politicians now speak of introducing foreign languages in kindergarten.

The second cause for my optimism about the future of the French economy is the recent legislation enacted by the government to open up business. Since 1945, France has had price controls, but companies have now been given the freedom to establish their own prices. In the area of fund transfers, with the exception of one or two years, French people and companies have always been under strict exchange control; the government has lifted this control, making it possible for companies to invest in foreign countries. In my opinion, this is a condition necessary for growth.

Fiscal measures should improve business. Following the examples of the United States and the United Kingdom, the French government has lowered corporate taxes from 50 percent to 42 percent, a savings of 11 billion French francs that companies can now invest in R&D or expansion. The reduction of individual tax rates, the top rate dropping from 65 percent to 58.5 percent, should stimulate both savings and consumer spending.

In general, France has been successfully fighting inflation. Our inflation rate for industrial products is the same as that of Germany, which is no small feat. Costs have increased less in France than in Germany during the last two years.

The final legislative action that has contributed to the increasingly good economic picture in France is the privatization program. Privatization of several large, previously nationalized companies has been so successful that, in some cases, the number of shares permitted per investor has had to be limited. The number of stockholders in France has doubled, which should have a favorable effect on the business climate as a whole.

All of these achievements demonstrate that France has one major objective: to ensure that French industry will be competitive with that of its neighbors in the coming years. In 1987, GNP growth of 2 percent was a bit better than predicted, and the budget deficit decreased. However, we have not yet solved our employment problems, which will be alleviated only by continued growth. The European Monetary System is working and, in my opinion, should be extended to the other industrialized nations. Stabilization of currencies will make it easier to manage companies and therefore further help us to improve our economic position.

The future looks bright for France if we can stay on the same course. Demographically, for once, we are at an advantage, since the French population will be greater than the West German population in the year 2000 or soon thereafter. If the French modify their "Gaulois" genes that prevent them from working well together, France can, with consistent efforts, become the first industrial nation in Europe. But we should no longer be speaking of individual nations. Rather, we should look forward to Europe as a whole becoming a strong partner for the United States. The twenty-first century need not be that of the Pacific Basin: It will be the century of global exchange.

Prologue

Judith Frommer and Janice McCormick

The picture painted by Jacques Maisonrouge in his foreword of a strong, economically driven French society looking confidently toward a global future is, as he indicates, not one necessarily familiar to Americans. A recent evolution has occurred in France, and previous assumptions and constants on which Americans have based their views and opinions about France and the French no longer hold true. In the past decade, France has undergone a political, economic, and cultural upheaval that has affected not only the way the French do business but also the way they think about it.

This evolution is the subject of *Transformations in French Business*. The critical date for that evolution is 1981, when the governing majority passed from the liberal leadership of Giscard to the Socialist Mitterrand. For business, this transition brought greater state intervention in the economy. Massive social transfers were made and nine major industrial groups and all banks were nationalized as the Socialists brandished antibusiness slogans. Under the previous liberal government, profitability and investments had declined; but now firms were threatened with a further erosion of their financial position.

The Socialist euphoria did not last long. Socialist public policy makers were forced to reconsider policies that had resulted in a weakened franc, budget deficits, a growing trade imbalance, and the continued rise of unemployment in spite of state aid. After 1983, the government underwent a massive policy reversal. The Socialists discovered the harsh realities of competition in global markets: To create jobs, export, and lower deficits, France would have to have more competitive companies. This meant that French market rigidities in both labor and trade would have to be eased; social costs to companies would have to be lowered; and "lame duck" companies would no longer be sheltered by the state.

France's Socialist leaders began to speak the language of business and to praise entrepreneurship. The old left-wing alternative, just as the old right-wing one before it, had failed to help France adapt to the post–oil crisis world. As ideological politics have become illegitimate, French society has undergone a change in its prevailing values; the nation seems to have discovered the virtues of business. Many of our essays document these cultural changes: the rise of interest in business schools and a growing number of business school students, the decline of private sector trade unionism, and a new breed of young managers.

In 1986, the center-right was returned to power in the parliamentary elections. Mitterrand and his right-wing Prime Minister, Jacques Chirac, are governing France in a "cohabitation." But there is more continuity than change from the previous government. Chirac has led the privatization of the companies that the Socialists had nationalized four years before, but he has met little opposition. This policy has few opponents, and for the first time the French population has rushed to purchase stock in the newly privatized companies. Politicians no longer debate the legitimacy of private business and competition.

Transformations in French Business: 1981–1987 is our attempt to introduce an English-speaking audience to this evolution. We present a view of France rarely offered to this audience: Representatives of the French business community along with a few senior-level civil servants speak directly to the non-French in an effort to explain, interpret, and defend the changes Mr. Maisonrouge has previewed.

This book is based on a collection of papers and presentations given at a colloquium at Harvard University in March 1987, entitled "French Business in 1987: New Directions or Old?" The aim of the colloquium was not only to inform but also to promote understanding. For this reason, rather than having foreign scholars analyze France from an outsider's point of view, the conference organizers invited the French participants to talk about themselves to an American audience, thus allowing debate and discussion between two groups that infrequently have a chance to exchange ideas.

The various seminars and panel discussions, while providing information about the current state of French business, developed the concept of business in a broader sociological framework. The papers in this collection present the writers' personal views in a relaxed, comprehensible style addressed to a general public. Their statements are unofficial and subjective; they are not necessarily telling you what is happening but what they think is happening. In some cases the authors do not agree, and when the discussion from the conference is included, you will note that the audience also did not always agree with the speakers.

The editors let the participants speak for themselves, grouping the papers without analyses, explanations, or summaries. We have, however, provided a thorough chronology as well as a glossary to aid those readers who are unfamiliar with key dates and terms. In addition, from time to time, we interject commentary to present background information or to provide missing links between various elements, showing how they relate to each other to form a whole. We have eschewed uniformity, preferring instead that the reader pursue an individual path through what we hope will be a fruitful and interesting exploration of the multiple facets of French business. Most fittingly, the journey begins with ''Perceptions and Realities.''

N.B.: Articles in this collection refer to events during Mitterrand's first term as president of France, May 1981 to May 1988.

Acknowledgments

The editors wish to thank the Harvard Business School, Division of Research, and the Georges Lurcy Charitable and Educational Trust whose generous support has made this book possible. We would also like to express our appreciation to Barbara Feinberg for her translations and editorial advice and to Rita Perloff for her tireless efforts in producing the manuscript. Finally, we acknowledge the cosponsors of the colloquium on which this book is based: the Department of Romance Languages and Literatures of Harvard University, and the Alliance Française of Boston-Cambridge, under the direction of Elaine Uzan Leary.

Transformations
in French Business

Introduction

French Business: Perceptions and Realities in the United States

Claude LeGal and Jean Lévy

CLAUDE LEGAL: There is a tremendous gap between the facts concerning French business in this country and the way it is generally perceived. Is such a misunderstanding unusual or abnormally surprising? In fact, no. Problems of perceptions between nations are frequent. But what strikes me most is how much this gap exists when you refer to France and the United States, and how much it has an impact on all our relations in politics, economy, trade, culture, and even mutual psychological perceptions. You will have to forgive first or to forget, as you prefer, that I am a French civil servant. I work in this country and I love it, and I love New York. I will say what I really feel.

France and French business are widely ignored here or misunderstood. I will try to develop three points. First, France as a whole is not correctly perceived. Second, the same is true for French business. Third, recent developments could narrow the gap, and many efforts are made or are going to be made to improve the situation.

First point: France is not easily understood in the United States, for a number of reasons. History, for instance. France is an old nation, and the past weighs heavily for us. For our American friends we refer too often to symbols, such as Lafayette or the Statue of Liberty, which correspond to a world of which France was a major part, a world which is now remote. Since then, it has gone the other way around. This "good old liberty" was brought back to France by the GIs in 1918 and in 1945, and so whenever we speak about a historical debt, for American people it means a recent French debt towards America, not the contrary. In fact, our attitude leads American people to think that we are ungrateful and chauvinistic.

The same is true for modern international politics. French foreign policy is frequently misinterpreted. American people often make decisions on a day-today basis, groping for facts the best they can, without referring constantly to history. Since America is young and powerful, its policy can be simple and even schematic; for example, fighting against Communism. But for such a small and old country as France, things are much more complicated. Americans do not appreciate the remaining consequences of our colonial responsibilities in Africa, or in Arab countries, for example. They don't take our nuclear power seriously, and even if they encourage European cooperation, they don't understand our European quarrels, as if French, English, and German, for example, could easily work together after centuries of wars.

We may say it is even worse as far as French internal politics are concerned. Americans do not easily understand what we call "cohabitation," and they are reluctant to admit the ideological basis of some among our political parties. But in fact, isn't your Republican president engaging in cohabitation with a Democratic Congress? And we should mention that French conservatives are closer and closer to American Republicans, and at the same time French Socialists do not differ so much anymore from the Democrats.

Another point concerns the French way of living. Americans very often consider as old-fashioned some fundamental values of French social life: family ties, the region you were born in, or where you live. These ties are responsible for rivalries between characters, dialects, and provinces. They keep people from easily accepting moves from one place to another as readily as Americans do. More generally, the search for well being, quiet good living, honor, and respect are frequently preferred to self-accomplishment, success, and money.

JEAN LÉVY: At this point, I would like to say something. Speaking from experience, during my four years in this country, I think that it is very difficult for a country like France to change its image. France has an image in which culture, fashion, wine, cosmetics, fragrances, and so on, are more important than anything else. It's part of the French image, it's part of the French fun, it's part of the French way of life. I have learned in marketing and advertising that it's easier to cultivate the strong points than to try to fight against the weak points. France's strong points are not technological; it's not technology, it's enjoying life, culture, having wonderful castles, nice houses, nice villages, and good food. Even if France has shown and proved to be a country with technology—and we will come back to that—I think that it's difficult to counterbalance the strong impression we have given through the years. And when you see Japan or Germany, I am not saying that they have no culture; they both have culture, but this culture is not shown as much and understood as much. I'm not saying that they are not enjoying life; they enjoy life, but I remember that the Germans said *wie Gott in Frankreich* (France is heaven on earth), and it's easier for them, not having the same kind of background, to show their technological image. France's only way, if we want to discuss technology, is to prove it product by product, and not to try as a country to show that we are technological, because it's a kind of a battle that can be lost easily.

LEGAL: Another point of misunderstanding. The fundamental French policy regarding social protection and promotion is widely ignored in the United States, or only considered in its negative and costly effects. American newspapers, at least on the East Coast, refer sometimes to our difficulties coping with the deficit of our social security system, but they almost never mention that medical care is almost entirely free in France. Americans criticize French universities, but they generally ignore the fact that the State is responsible for expenses, and consequently, studies are extremely inexpensive and available to everyone.

In work relations, the French social aims and certain ideological orientations of our trade unions are frequently misunderstood too. The mechanisms of labor negotiations inside companies (*comités d'entreprise, délégués du personnel*) and the role of the labor inspectors whose main goal is worker protection appear to be excessively complicated. Criticism is fierce against our strikes, and for example against the CGT (Confédération Générale du Travail), the Communist-oriented union. But the Mafia influence in the United States, your closed shop system, and the domination of the Teamsters do not exist in France.

The last issue concerns the functioning of our business world. Living in the United States, I quite understand Americans' confusion when they read about our successive nationalizations and privatizations, our policies regarding prices and currencies, the "undercapitalization" of our firms, the low levels of profits, the importance of the state in business life, and the fact that the priority of the French elite is to be a civil servant or technocrat rather than a businessman or lawyer, as is the case here.

Regarding French business and its perception in the United States, I will give some examples, some possible explanations, and a major problem: a question of methods. The French-American Foundation and *L'Express* organized an opinion poll in April 1986 that produced, among others, the following results: One U.S. citizen out of two is not convinced that France, and I quote, "is a leading country in the field of medicine." Only two to three Americans out of ten agree with the following three statements: "France is among the leading industrial countries in the world"; "France is a serious competitor for the United States in the field of aerospace industry"; "France has a strong nuclear force of its own." Very few among my American friends or visitors know that France is the fourth-largest exporter in the world and that we are now leading Japan in export per capita. Few people know that 59.4 percent of the U.S. imports of French products are elaborated industrial products: aircraft, engines, chemistry specialties, and auto parts. On the contrary, sometimes the cliches are surprisingly more in our favor than they are in reality. For example, to the question "When you think of French products, what are the products that come to mind immediately?" The answers are 84.7 percent, champagne and wines; 80.7 percent, clothing and shoes. This last figure has to be compared to the fact that unfortunately, in spite of our reputation, less than 1.5 percent of women's apparel in the United States is imported from France. Why such confusion? Because in big East Coast cities, French-sounding trademarks are employed to sell foreign or domestic products to take advantage of the French brand appeal. Some examples of that kind could be mentioned in the cosmetics and perfume business as well as in the wine sector.

LÉVY: It's true. But to come back to this point, I have a study here about the French apparel business and why it is not successful in the United States. One of the reasons Claude LeGal gave is the development of American brands that appear French, and you have a lot of them, but this is competition. But you see also that the Italians are very successful in the States, much more successful than the French, and this is not a question of American competition. It's another question. A study was made last year to understand the lack of success of the French industry in the fashion business in the States. Some excerpts: "The present mentality of the French managers in the fabric business is not oriented to exportation. They believe that it is very difficult to work with the United States, and nobody is sure to be successful. It's a kind of demobilization of the French people and French companies because there is a lack of professionalism among most of the French companies in this kind of field."

What kind of difficulties, what kind of problems did they encounter? Number one, you need to have an export service and someone speaking English. If you don't have that, planning cannot work, customs rules are ignored, and you don't know how to finance. Very few of the French textile companies—apparel and fabric-producing—have a subsidiary or even a licensee in the States. They have people who come here from time to time, but they don't have a permanent organization. Very few of them have a showroom to present their products, and that doesn't help to make French brands known. French people, when they come to the States, go to New York; very few of them go to Dallas or to Los Angeles, and the competitors are going there. The French products are not always adapted to the American market. Very few efforts are made to modify the sizes, the colors, or even the fibers. The Americans like "hot" colors, even sometimes for men's clothes. "Frenchmen," says an American specialist, "don't like to take risks, to surprise the consumer, they are too classical." Valentino, for example, or Giorgio Armani, are presenting real clothes adapted to the American market.

The French are sometimes as imperialist as the Americans can be. And they believe what is good for France should be wonderful for the United States. The French have considered the U.S. market as exportation from France, without taking American tastes into consideration. The collections that are presented are too large. I remember a fashion show in July 1986, where the French did not select among the names of the designers, and they didn't select among the clothes the designers were showing. The collections lasted for hours, and it was the hottest day of the year, so you can imagine how the people were reacting—the journalists, *Harper's* and so on. When the Italians come, they have real shows and they have a selection, and it lasts an hour or an hour and a half; they really have the clothes that are adapted to the U.S. market.

I have been talking about a bad example, and I could develop it a lot, but it shows one point that I would like to elaborate now. We have to develop much more real marketing science in France. There are a lot of marketing specialists around here, even coming from France, in advertising also, but marketing is not to produce and to sell after; it's first to understand the needs of the consumer, of the country you have to fight with. We are export-minded, we are one of the biggest exporters in the world, but for many companies, export is a way to go when the national market cannot absorb the production. It's not something organized as part of the international strategy of a company.

Second, when you want to export, you have to study and again to know the need. One point I would like to raise is historical: France is not a country with merchant education. Someone said that France is a country of clerks, peasants, and engineers—I added engineers. The engineers—and I worked some years ago in French groups and associations that tried to develop marketing and to find out new ways to redeploy French industry—I appreciate engineers; I don't always understand them—that's why I appreciate them—but I believe that if you give the power inside a company to too many engineers, the power to manage, the power to develop strategy—engineers have a good understanding of quality but they do not have a good understanding of competition. The best quality is not always the way to compete. You have to find a way to adapt quality to the price and to the service. And with too much perfection in quality, you can be out of the market because of too high a price. You can be out of the market because sometimes the best quality is not what the consumer is looking for, and in this field we have to learn a lot, not to take the engineers out of the companies—we need engineering, we need research—but to build a marketing sense and the sales sense which is becoming more and more important, more and more real, but which is still not accepted in a lot of companies.

On a similar note, I believe that one of the reasons of the success in this country of women in high positions is because you believe in commercial functions. What I mean and what I'm seeing every day: The success of women is the success of individuals who are wonderful salespeople, who are very committed, and believe in the products they are selling. The sales function in this country is a major one. You are sales minded; in Europe, not today, but yesterday, when I wanted to hire and when I wanted to promote someone as a *directeur commercial* of a company, the person asked me not to put "commercial" on his business card because the commercial function in Europe implies someone who has failed, who has no education. So I think the problem is not between men and women; in this country you believe in a question of commercial functions, and women are very successful in commercial functions again because they believe in the product, they have a lot of faith, they are committed, they are wonderful negotiators. It's the same in finance because again it's commercial functions; and the success of women in finance is because they are wonderful salespeople, and you don't have this kind of function in Europe today.

Marketing and advertising are sometimes considered as jokes or as narcissistic for the chairman of the company. But they are part of a strategy, and not only specialists of marketing and of international sales, but those trained as engineers or as managers must accept this.

LeGal: I have tried to find some explanation for this inadequate situation of our image. We should consider separately the image within the business community and the overall general opinion. We notice that the nonspecialized, less-educated people in the United States have the worst image of our products. This is encouraging because on the contrary, better-educated Americans express more positive views about France and French products. As for the overall opinion, we suffer from a strange gap that is not in our favor. Between commonly known French traditional products, for example, the "three F's"—food, fashion, and fragrance—on one side, and the high-tech equipment on the other—aircraft engines, nuclear plants—we have few products able to build the image we need among nonspecialists.

What kind of products am I referring to? Mass distribution products, products that people physically touch or use frequently, products having a rather tangible high level of technology. Some examples are cars from Germany and Japan; cameras, stereos, generally from Japan. I would like also to mention a paradox. We're suffering from an image of excess of sophistication. For example, high-tech products from France are often too complicated and too fragile. Some of our cars talk, but I'm not sure they run. Our dishwashers are much more modern than American ones, but when their programming system fails, they become useless. I've been told that American housewives are not as modern as we think; they want big old cars, they want a big solid dishwasher that works. Buyers are not necessarily technicians. As for fashion and luxury products, we are very often a model from which copies are made in Hong Kong or Taiwan, but Hermès, Christofle, Givenchy sell only to an elite, and lower-quality products made in France won't be able to compete very often.

Sophistication: Perhaps Americans see us as intellectuals, even mandarins, whose influence is mainly in the field of literature and culture. It appears that our reputation as a sophisticated, intellectual people has a negative influence on our mass distribution and everyday-quality products. Sophistication or high technological level brings us a good reputation among the elite and specialists who, by definition, are few and have a limited influence. But if American aeronautical engineers, optical specialists, and telecommunication technicians know that French technology ranks high, we should be able to take advantage of their opinion to promote our production better.

Regarding a lack of methods. We cannot be exhaustive here. I'll only mention classic criticism and look for some explanation again. The French are good engineers, but they are not sufficiently market-minded. Good firms really exist in France with good marketing reliability, good trade relations, but they are not very numerous. Why do the French have a poor reputation in business? External trade is still a novelty for many French firms, who give priority to French internal markets. Social promotion in France means being an engineer, high civil servant, professor, but never a successful businessman. Business organization is frequently insufficient.

Lévy: At this point, I can give an example from recent personal experience. One of the most upscale French shoe companies wanted to open a store in New York as a kind of showcase. They opened it about six months ago. To open this store they hired a French advertising agency which dealt from Paris and managed the advertising and promotion for this store from Paris. These people, operating out of Paris, didn't know anything about the behavior of U.S. customers; they didn't know anything about promotional competition. Why did they hire this French organization instead of hiring an American firm? Because the French organization said it had correspondents in the States, but it didn't use them. Another point: The French people who manage this company didn't appoint someone to be the boss in New York. They had the salesman in the store, but this salesman was selling. He didn't know anything about advertising, promotions; it was not his job. So they decided to send another person each month to New York to find out what wasn't working and to manage the person in the store and to work with the French advertising agency. I live in New York; I'm a shareholder of this company, so I got worried, and I had them find someone in France able to understand the United States, who has been in the United States, who would accept staying some months here to run the store, and I helped them find the promotional organization, but they lost hundreds of thousands of dollars during the first six months by this kind of misunderstanding, which is crazy but which happens quite often.

LeGal: A last remark and maybe a cliche. We have a general problem of mentality: The French are generally considered more brilliant than serious.

Lévy: And arrogant.

LeGal: And arrogant. Fine. Well it's difficult to rebut this cliche, partly true, partly excessively unfavorable. Some remarks: Our cultural image does not make business life so easy, it gives us a reputation of being dreamers. In fact we look for individual originality. I think it's the key to understanding the French. But originality is not easily compatible with organization. And lastly, I think there is also an emotional problem. You love or you hate French people. It complicates cool and efficient business relations.

Lévy: On this point again, I had two experiences as a businessman in the United States. *Women's Wear Daily*—you may know this magazine which puts pressure on the industry to know what's going on—wanted to have news of a business deal first, and I didn't want to have the news coming out before it was really signed, so I refused. The head of the daily newspaper gave me a call and said "Ah! You are like all the Frenchmen, you are arrogant!" I still don't understand today why, but it's part of a cliche. I can understand sometimes why, but it's part of a cliche, and it's a cliche we have to fight against. Maybe we are arrogant; maybe sometimes it's a misunderstanding and the love-hate relationship you were talking about.

Another story concerns our acquisition of an American company. We had

around $450 million in sales—I'm talking about three years ago—and we ac-
quired a division of Warner Communications, a $150 million business. It was
really an experience to see the fears of the Americans to be acquired by a French
company, even in the cosmetics business, which is one of our specialties. So I
tried to study, because as a marketing man, I wanted to know the fears in order
to counterbalance them. First fear: The French don't believe in organizational
charts; even if they have them, they don't believe in them and they are not real.
So I knew that I had to have an organization chart. Second: The French promise,
but they never keep their promises. When they talk about salaries, when they
talk about not firing people, they never tell the truth, they're always lying. France
is a country where people lie and never respect their image. What I can say is
that the merger went well. It took us two years to be successful and to quiet
down and not to fire people, and so on, and today, there is no problem. But I
remember a dinner in the first weeks where the atmosphere between the U.S.
people who had been acquired and the French people who were at the top of
the organization was very cool, even cold. It didn't last long, but there were
many fears because we have an image of bureaucracy, an image of not respecting
an organization chart, an image as people who use what we call *le système D*
in French, which means never standing in line, and so on and so forth. And it's
a big fight. When you are part of an organization that has been successful
worldwide, to absorb an American company is a very big fight; it's very difficult.

LeGal: I feel my job is not so easy because I have to be a diplomat. I have
to say that I agree with Jean but have to demonstrate the contrary, you know.
So am I pessimistic? In fact, I'm convinced that in the present situation the gaps
are narrowing. France is changing. France is becoming more politically comprehensible for the United States. We have no more Communists in the government. French Socialists are becoming Social Democrats. Since March 1986,
the Conservative government headed by Jacques Chirac is practicing a kind of
Reaganism. In the economy, big firms are coming back to the private sector—
privatization. We also have our deregulation—*déréglementation*—no more price
controls and no more currency exchange control. Our inflation is down to an
annual rate of roughly 2 percent to 3 percent. We are reducing public expenditure,
the budget of the state, and subsidies at the same time as we are beginning to
reduce taxes. Our monetary policy is no longer as erratic. The currencies are
linked inside the European community by the European monetary system. In
business, France is now open to foreign investments. France is turning away
from protectionism and is now widely open to commercial competition. The
profits are magnified since March 1986, and the French stock exchange is boom-
ing, though not as much as the Dow Jones. The influence of the trade unions is
decreasing. The influence of U.S. business in France is considerable. U.S.
investments in France are $7.8 billion at the present time. Entrepreneurial culture
coming from America is becoming very important in France. The frenzy among
young students to obtain an American MBA is on the upsurge in France.

Also, in the United States, the business position of France is becoming important. I would say France is consolidating its partnership in the United States even if only on a modest level. Imports from France are approximately 3 percent of total U.S. imports. French investments in the United States are $6.3 billion compared with $3.7 billion in 1980. Big investments are developing recently from France toward the United States: Rhône-Poulenc, Union Carbide, Agrochemistry, Yves St. Laurent, Charles of the Ritz, CGE, ITT, Air Liquide, for example; and the French technological presence is increasing.

This second idea is that a new kind of French and Franco-American community is appearing over here. Eight hundred French firms have 1,300 subsidiaries in the United States. We had only 1,000 subsidiaries in 1984 and 400 in 1980. These subsidiaries are often managed by young bicultural French entrepreneurs with an average age of 40, an MBA, and no complex regarding the United States. This community is no longer afraid of American business life and is now trying to change, in an American way, the marketing policies of their own French parent firms. These developments are giving us good results in the United States from both big and small firms. Some examples: Perrier, which is now an American brand; Cosmair, Lectra System, Möet-Hennessy, Chandon, Thomson, Cristal d'Arcques, Danone, Baccarat, etc.

LÉVY: I want to make one more point. I share Claude's point of view completely. There has been a very big change in France, and I think that the younger people who are traveling internationally much more, having a better understanding of foreign languages, who ignore borders and who are more entrepreneurially minded represent the opportunity of France today and of France tomorrow. And I also believe that the Comité Maisonrouge, which is the Comité Image de la France, will be a way to show the Americans, through seminars, through development of awareness of the successful French technological products, that there is a new way of developing an understanding of French technology, of French industry, in the States. Again first, because I think the younger people are part of this kind of fight ten times more than the older generation and second, because today France is aware that internationalization and export are part of strategy, and not simply something you do when business is bad.

LEGAL: Just two words of conclusion. Understanding between France and the United States is a tough problem. We ought to keep in mind the scale of the two countries. France is more active worldwide per capita than the United States, and there are nearly five times more Americans in the world than Frenchmen, and your GDP is more than five times greater than ours. France is linked to parts of the world, such as Africa and Arab countries, at a time when your priorities are Israel, Nicaragua, or the Philippines. France acts within the EEC and in cooperation with Germany, Italy, Great Britain, and others; we have no such independence as you naturally enjoy. Problems of mutual perceptions are real, and we intend to deal with these difficulties not as intellectuals but as concerned business partners.

LÉVY: I would like to say something about European and American management. I was asked one year ago to organize a summer seminar at one of the most well-known American universities on the difference between European and American management. I sat down and I tried to find a way. I didn't find any. I believe it's a difference of people. You have managers in the United States who are integrating some of what we call European humanism, and you have lots of European managers who have been educated in U.S. universities who are creating Anglo-Saxon efficiency. I don't believe today that we could say that there is a European management style compared to an American management style. When I read *In Search of Excellence* and when I think of the books in Europe that came out of French organizations, not selling as well as the U.S. books, I ask myself, what's happening in reality? I think it is as difficult in the States as in Europe to compare ideas to realities; it takes years, but I don't believe in the need for seminars. The other point I want to raise concerns one of the questions. Never forget that it has always been easier for French companies, even a large one—and I'm thinking of mine, which is number one in the world today in the cosmetics industry—it has always been easier for us to sell to Latin countries than to Anglo-Saxons because the link was much more natural. It was easier for us to do business in Latin America than in Germany; it was easier for us to do business in Spain than in Sweden. It's only in the last twenty or thirty years that we started to fight to increase our presence in the Anglo-Saxon market; there was a kind of fear of entering this sort of market because the atmosphere was not the same, and it is the same with French exports. Why is France, the fourth richest country in the world today, not as strong as it should be? The same is true for investment. And we are more oriented to Africa, we are more oriented to Latin America because it was a natural link. So it is something that is shifting today, but it takes time.

EDITORS' REMARKS

This exchange between Claude LeGal, a French civil servant, and Jean Lévy, a French businessman, sets the stage for what is to follow. They raise themes that were explored in greater depth by other participants at the March 1987 Harvard colloquium on French business from which the following papers were drawn.

First, like these two commentators, other participants questioned the image of France in the United States; the theme of mutual misunderstandings and misperceptions runs through many of the chapters that follow. The popular American image of France is that of a contentious polity with ideological parties, an anticapitalist, class-ridden society, and an unproductive state-led economy famous only for the three F's—fashion, fragrance, and food. As we shall see, if this image was ever true, the current state of affairs is far more complex.

A second theme we found in all of the comments was the coexistence of continuity and change within the same nation. Though the contributors disagree on what has changed and its pervasiveness and permanence, they each have witnessed aspects of a new society more favorable to business. In each of the chapters of this book, the conference participants describe a new business climate that has swept over France in the past ten years changing the way they do business.

Our report of the conference proceedings begins with macroeconomic policy where we examine what has changed in French trade. Tordjman and Vilgrain use examples of trade relations with the United States and French food and agricultural policy to paint a picture of France as an industrial exporter and an integral part of Europe.

But can we say that France has undergone a business revolution? In economic policy, there has been an important change of direction. Even the French Socialist Party and President Mitterrand are now preaching the gospel of entrepreneurship, privatization, and the free market. In Chapter two, Bellanger and Blanchard agree on the importance of political institutional changes and the emergence of a broader social consensus around more liberal policy measures, but they disagree on the impact of liberal policies on French economic performance. Angé and Carreras continue the debate with a discussion of the revolution in French business investment. With a surprising array of foreign strategies and domestic investment instruments, French companies have more possibilities open to them than ever before.

But will managers be able to seize these opportunities, unhampered by state controls? Loyrette and Barret argue that the new state policy of privatization of the many nationalized companies is proof of the state's willingness to allow managers greater freedom to manage their own companies. Their confidence is admirable, but the process and the speed of privatization of French companies is, nonetheless, tightly controlled by the state.

Within France, the image of business has also changed. In Parts three and four, we look at the increased legitimacy of business in French society. Ten years ago, "profit" was a dirty word; this is no longer true. As Boissonnat points out, dozens of new business publications have emerged and are selling well. Marcus and Beaudoin, respectively heads of two leading French advertising and public relations agencies, tell us that active public relations campaigns and quality advertising have become critical to companies' successful performance. The changes in the French society are even reflected in the market for luxury goods. Doucet describes for us how that market has been democratized or "vulgarized" as a broader spectrum of French citizens seek luxury goods or at least the appearance of luxury.

Finally, our participants saw change in French social relations. According to Livian, trade unions have moderated their ideologies, and relations at work have become more participatory; Dautresme and Bonnet indicate that women are taking a more active role in work and society; and Larçon and Dufour argue that the brightest French students who once would have scorned management, preferring to become civil servants, are now seeking management degrees and jobs in the private sector. These social changes have affected workplace relations. Impatient with bureaucratic companies and seniority-based promotions, today's young French managers have a new style, are more international, and dream of creating their own companies, according to Daniel Jouve.

Yet, there are still roadblocks to the "new France." French companies still have difficulty marketing and selling their products; the state still plays an active role in setting the rules of competition; and we cannot be certain that the nation's new liberal faith will survive a major economic reversal, such as another oil crisis or a stock market crash. Yet we believe that these changes in French business are significant enough to let our participants speak of their own experiences and present to you the "new France."

PART I

French Trade Relations
since 1981

I

Relations with the United States

Jean-Daniel Tordjman

Since the Second World War, the United States and France have been among the four major exporters in the world. In 1986, the United States became the second-largest worldwide exporter, after Germany; France ranked fourth, behind Japan but ahead of the United Kingdom and Italy. Yet, despite the two countries' overall trade performance, until recently, bilateral trade between them has remained surprisingly limited. Traditionally, France has traded primarily with other European countries and French-speaking African nations, whereas the United States's major trade partners have been its neighbors—Canada and Mexico—and more recently, Japan. Not until the period 1980–1985 did trade between France and the United States substantially increase. Today, the United States is the fifth-largest export market for France, and France is the seventh-largest market for the United States.

This overview of French-American trade relations will cover three areas: macroeconomic factors affecting the two countries' trade relations, the principal characteristics of the trade flow, and the major trade disputes between France and the United States.

MACROECONOMIC FACTORS

In general, there are two principal macroeconomic influences on trade relations: the differential in the growth of aggregate demand between two countries; and the international competitiveness of each economy, which in turn depends upon the value of its currency, relative production costs, and productivity level. Specifically for French-American trade relations, from 1980 to 1987, the macroeconomic influences were, first, the high growth rate of U.S. domestic demand relative to that of France and other industrial countries (see Exhibit 1). This

Exhibit 1
Real Domestic Demand in Selected Industrial Countries

Index, 1982 = 100

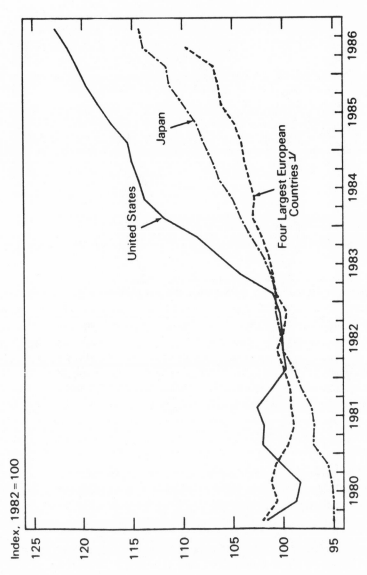

1/ France, Italy, United Kingdom, and West Germany, weighted by GNP.

Note.—Domestic demand is the sum of personal consumption expenditures, gross private domestic investment, and government purchases of goods and services.

Sources: Department of Commerce and country sources.

growth was due to the U.S. budget deficit, which rose dramatically after 1980, and to an increasing marginal propensity to consume. Since 1983, French economic growth has consistently been lower than that of the United States, and this sluggishness has encouraged French companies to look for foreign markets. The second macroeconomic factor has been the French franc/U.S. dollar exchange rate, which fluctuated widely in this period. The rate per dollar went from FF 4.25 in 1979 to FF 10.60 in February 1985, then dropped to FF 5.5 in December 1987.

If we divide the period into three stages, we can see how the factors have interacted.

1980–1982	France faced a large overall trade deficit, particularly with the United States. The effect of the rising dollar on French trade was offset by the country's expansionary fiscal policy during these years.
1983–1985	The French trade position toward the United States improved dramatically as a result of the dollar's continued appreciation and the continued growth of American domestic demand, which was relatively higher than that of France.
1986–1987	The bilateral trade movement reversed and progressively worsened for France as a result of the dollar's decrease in value and a slight reduction in American domestic demand growth. This situation should last for at least a few more years because the high level of the U.S. trade and budget deficits may require a further decrease in demand growth.

CHARACTERISTICS OF THE TRADE FLOW

There are three primary characteristics of French-American trade: trade volume, trade balance, and trade structure.

Volume

Trade between France and the United States until the beginning of this decade was significantly lower than its potential. Moreover, until 1980, the high value of the franc relative to the dollar impeded French access to the U.S. market, which was already considered complex, highly competitive, and too large.

Between 1980 and 1986, volume increased spectacularly: French exports to the United States grew from FF 21 billion in 1980 ($5 billion at a 4.23 franc/dollar exchange rate) to FF 61 billion in 1986 ($8.82 billion at a 6.93 exchange rate). There are currently just under 1,000 French companies with at least one subsidiary in the United States, twice as many as in 1980. In 1986, however, for the first time since 1975, trade diminished relative to the previous year: French exports to the United States dropped by FF 14 billion (down 19 percent),

Exhibit 2
French Trade Balance with the United States and French Franc/Dollar Exchange Rate, 1980–1986

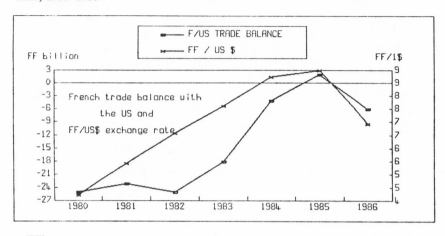

while U.S. exports to France fell by FF 6 billion (down 8.4 percent). The dollar's decline was partly responsible for this decrease. In 1985–1986, the dollar depreciated 23 percent, leading to a 14 percent reduction in the value of French exports to the United States because 60 percent of these exports were denominated in dollars. This direct effect accounted for 75 percent of the total decrease. In 1987, trade continued to be reduced, but the rate slowed.

Balance

From World War I to 1977, France suffered a structural trade deficit with the United States; from 1977 to 1982, this deficit tripled, reaching $3.85 billion in 1982. In 1980, the ratio of French exports to the United States to French imports from the United States was only 46 percent and increased to 57 percent by 1982.

Since 1982, an improvement in the French trade balance has led to a slight surplus in 1985, for the first time since 1959. However, according to French statistics—as opposed to U.S. statistics—France incurred a deficit in 1986, which increased in 1987. Differences in French and U.S. statistics occur because of an overvaluation of French imports from the United States by 5 percent to 10 percent (mainly in antiques and fissile products) and an undervaluation of French exports to the United States by 20 percent (primarily in the agriculture and computer industries).

As Exhibit 2 demonstrates, the links between the franc-dollar exchange rate and the French trade balance with the United States are clear.

Structure

While remaining strong in traditional French areas like wine and luxury goods, French sales to the United States have recently and rapidly changed in favor of high-technology products. Sixty percent of total exports consisted of manufactured goods in 1986, in contrast to 45 percent in 1976. The top French exports to the United States are not wine or perfume (although France has 37 percent of the world market in perfume) but aeronautics, including airplanes, aircraft engines, and parts; this accounts for one-fifth of total French exports to the United States. In fact, France is the United States's largest foreign supplier of aerospace products.

The second-largest French export sector is the food industry (12 percent of the total), particularly wine, spirits, and champagne. Two other industries, automobiles and nuclear products, were strong but have subsequently declined. Other French exports to the United States are organic chemicals, steel products, and construction equipment.

American exports to France include manufactured goods (70 percent of the total), and the chief export sector is aeronautics, which accounts for 17.7 percent. The second-largest export sector is the computer industry, with 16.7 percent of total exports. These two sectors account for more than one-third of all exports, although other significant sectors include electronics, food products, and energy products.

TRADE DISPUTES

Two sectors are subject to French-American trade conflicts, and in both, French interests resemble those of other European countries. The first is agricultural goods, the second is aerospace.

The United States frequently criticizes the European Community's Common Agricultural Policy, but its arguments are not consistent with the facts. For example, it is held that Europe is a closed market. This is not correct: Europe is a major importer of farm products; these imports totaled $46 billion in 1986. Furthermore, EEC export subsidies are smaller than U.S. subsidies. In 1986, 11 million European farmers received $22 billion, whereas the 2.5 million American farmers received $26 billion. The U.S. farmer, on a *per capita* basis, then, receives much more aid than his EEC counterpart. In addition, the EEC is not a net exporter of agricultural products. In fact, Europe is running a deficit in this area of $20 billion. Finally, Europe is the primary importer of U.S. agricultural products, making it America's best customer.

The second trade issue pertains to aeronautics, particularly the Airbus. Airbus Industrie, a consortium of European manufacturers from four countries, has successfully challenged the monopoly the United States has enjoyed in the commercial aircraft field.

Once again, the popular belief in the United States is that the European aircraft market is closed, and once again, this is incorrect. There are 1,000 U.S. commercial aircraft flying in Europe today, compared to 60 European aircraft in the United States. The three main European countries involved in the Airbus consortium have collectively ordered nearly $10 billion worth of Boeing products. Moreover, 35 percent of Airbus' value is derived from the United States since 500 of 4,000 subcontractors are American. And finally, because military and civil research in aeronautics is linked, it is difficult to identfy public subsidies for commercial airplane construction clearly.

An exclusive focus on these two areas of dispute, however, is a misreading of trade relations between Europe and the United States. Although its increasing trade deficit is a grave concern for America and for the rest of the world, Europe is a major U.S. partner; further, the European market is at least as open as the U.S. market and is far more open than Asian markets generally and the Japanese market in particular. In addition, one-half of the U.S. trade deficit is with Asian countries; one-third is with Japan. Although the European-American trade balance is in favor of Europe—19 percent of the total U.S. deficit in 1986—the deficit compared to trade is very different, as the following demonstrates:

> *U.S. trade deficit as a percentage of U.S. exports*—
> to Japan: 216 percent; to the EEC: 49 percent

> *U.S. trade deficit as a percentage of U.S. imports*—
> from Japan: 68 percent; from the EEC: 33 percent

These numbers show that the level of the U.S. deficit with Japan is more than twice the level of U.S. exports to Japan, whereas the U.S. deficit with the EEC is only half the level of U.S. exports to the EEC.

The future will tell whether the 1982–1985 period was only an epiphenomenon in French-American trade relations.

As far as French exports to the United States are concerned, the present drop in the dollar is likely to make exporting to the United States more difficult for French firms. It may, however, induce them to improve their competitiveness, quality control, and technological performance. Further, the dollar's low value has led to a surge of French direct investment in the United States, especially in the distribution sector, where French presence has been insufficient. Given the U.S. market's size, French firms cannot afford to decrease their market share; in this regard, they can count on the support of the French Trade Commission in the United States.

Of course, the dollar's depreciation provides U.S. industry with outstanding opportunities to sell abroad, and in France particularly. U.S. exports to France in 1986–1987, denominated in dollars, have increased dramatically.

Protectionism is a danger that must be faced. It would only be counterproductive, prompt retaliation, and lead to an implosive cumulative process in international trade. Rather, Europe and the United States must remain partners in negotiations to eliminate trade barriers and fight together against unfair trade practices.

The goal for French and American firms is to adapt their worldwide export strategies to a new international environment that includes sharp competition from newly industrialized countries. Increased cooperation between our two countries would provide more opportunities for success, especially in research and development in high-technology sectors, where synergy is achievable. Over-all, in a world largely dominated by economic forces, trade cooperation is a top priority and the only way to promote prosperity in the Free World.

2

France, Trading Partner in Europe and the Third World

Jean-Louis Vilgrain

A brief historical review of France's geographical constraints is necessary to understand the country's situation today.

Historically, France's political policy has centered around the three fundamental components that result from its geopolitical and cultural borders: the Atlantic, Europe, and Africa. France has attempted to synthesize and reconcile these components, yet the policy sometimes becomes contradictory. Our colonial policy in the nineteenth century was undoubtedly detrimental to two of these components; in the same manner, decolonization favored these two components. Today, decolonization is finished. Cultural and commercial benefits from former colonies still remain, and the colonies have become sovereign partners with France. They represent what France considers to be the Third World. In a parallel sense, France wants to consolidate and enlarge the concept of Europe. So, there is often a contradiction between its political interests in the Third World and in Europe; sometimes the Atlantic is favored over the Mediterranean.

My intention here is to go beyond political divisions and see what is permanent in the geopolitical or geoeconomic behavior of my country. My vantage point is that of a French industrialist who watches political regimes pass. I have observed a permanent trend toward a political policy that is the result of a consensus among all political parties.

It is evident today that foreign policy unites the French. However, this new consensus does not prevent contradictions from appearing between European and Third World political positions. This is why it seems difficult to deal with the problems of France and Europe. I prefer to speak about a European France, a concept I shall define; then I shall examine its consequences with regard to the Third World, particularly, Africa.

EUROPEAN FRANCE

When it became a member of the Common Market, France agreed to transfer sovereignty, specifically affecting its relationship with the Third World, by permitting the Brussels Commission to sign the Lomé agreements in its name.

The Common Market exists and relations between the Third World and France have been defined by such agreements. Nevertheless, due to its past involvement in Africa, France has maintained and even consolidated what is called the *zone franc*. This means that France will stand as a financial guarantor for the currency in all the French-speaking countries from ex-French West Africa to French Equatorial Africa. This includes nearly all former colonies.

France is still part of the European Monetary System, however, and its responsibilities within the system no doubt consolidate the French franc but also tie its fate to all European currencies. Thus, indirectly, the definition of the Communauté Financière Africaine (CFA) franc is established through consultation with our partners in the Common Market. This is what England apparently refused to do in the case of the "zone sterling".

So, the different exchange components between European France and Third World countries are linked, because of exports and imports, to the Third World, and more precisely to Africa. The French trade balance is an example. We export a large quantity of agricultural products, manufactured goods, and arms. These are typical exports to a developing country. The same is true of the imported goods: We import raw materials and labor from our former colonies. Our imports from developed countries are primarily in the form of equipment. Thus, European France has nevertheless remained a traditional France linked historically with its former colonial partners.

One of the difficulties in carrying out European political policy in France is in the area that I know best: common agricultural policy. It is a political contradiction to manage between the guarantees that must be given to European farmers and the fact that the countries of the Third World can export to Europe a certain quantity of their products that may compete with European agricultural goods. This is especially true for protein-based agricultural goods, which compete with European dairy products. It is also true for citrus fruits.

Discussions and negotiations take place in the Common Market agricultural organization: the Common Agricultural Policy (CAP), under the Commission of the European Community. France is, of course, an influential member, but final decisions are made by the commission.

Thus, one cannot separate France from Europe. Except in certain areas, such as space, armaments, and atomic matters, France has delegated to the Common Market Commission its negotiation powers. In the same manner, the European Parliament's ratification of the "Unique Act" will lead in a short time to the unification of the European market. The French market will soon no longer exist.

Finally, trade variations are only a relatively weak cause of the monetary shifts we are currently facing; it is mainly the enormous shifting of capital that is a determining factor, and France participates just like the rest of Europe. This interesting contemporary phenomenon is full of upheavals that are both positive and negative for international trade, especially within Europe.

Let's take a slightly esoteric example, the compensatory payments, that were established for both relations within the communities and relations with third parties for products regulated by common agricultural policies. There is total freedom of capital exchange, and interest rates are more or less attractive depending upon the country. For a country to avoid devaluing its currency (a good financial operation, but a bad economic operation), it can play on the differences in interest rates. Only Switzerland, which does not belong to the Common Market, took measures to discourage incoming capital by setting negative or extremely low interest rates.

When France entered the European Monetary System, it integrated its monetary policy into the European policy. This, of course, poses problems with the CFA franc and thus with the Third World. France's position can be detailed through three types of problems that it confronts facing the Third World.

1. France and its former colonies as part of the Third World;

2. France and its former colonies as part of the *zone franc*;

3. France and the Third World exclusive of the two other cases.

The former colonies included in the *zone franc* are essentially the Maghreb countries. Here we come back to the geopolitical constant of France in relation to the Mediterranean, a vital and sensitive area for all of Europe. Exchanges are principally raw materials: oil, gas, and labor. French exports are basically in grains and some manufactured goods. However, in imports, especially in the oil-based products, such as olive oil, we find ourselves immediately in conflict with our Mediterranean partners, Italy and Spain. This is particularly true with Tunisia. Conflicts also arise in agro-industrial products like coffee and cocoa.

In our relations with the countries in the *zone franc* we have a very special case. This is the establishment of a monetary area, which is currently a unique situation in the world. There is a fixed parity between the French franc and the CFA franc, which is an element of stability for most of these countries. Such a situation is even stronger and more constraining because this parity is directly linked, as I have said, to the European Monetary System. This is reassuring for those who hold debt claims on Africa; it also expands freedom to transfer capital. However, it points up the contradiction of a national France that inherited its colonies and a European France. (By the way, the International Monetary Fund criticizes such a monetary zone and challenges its continuance.)

In fact, for Africans exporting products whose world market price is in dollars this represents an extreme handicap: The selling price is in dollars, while the production cost is linked to European currencies. Parity is strongly reduced in relation to other European currencies. In addition, for a number of years, there has been a differential inflation between France and French-speaking Africa, which has widened as the inflation rate weakens in Europe.

Therefore, having the CFA franc attached to the French franc, which in turn is linked to European currencies, is an extremely serious matter. It does not at all reflect the economic circumstances of Africa. These countries' exports and their profit-earning capacity are handicapped by having exports in dollars, even to European countries, and by the inflation differential with European countries. This penalizes the competitiveness of the African economy in relation to the Franco-European economy and creates a paradoxical situation like that of Portugal at the time of Salazar: a strong currency in a struggling economy.

Such a situation becomes even more paradoxical when, in spite of fixed parities between the French franc and the CFA franc in French and African exchanges, the European Community applies compensatory payments in agro-industrial exchanges.

The final implication between European France and the Third World exists outside of the two preceding points dealing with former colonies or the ex-franc area. Here, each country is a separate case. In economic aid agreements or others in the large international negotiations peripheral to the GATT negotiations, France cannot do everything it would like because it has delegated part of its power to the Common Market Commission. This is particularly true in the area of agricultural aid.

A rather precise example that touches on French and European relations with the United States is the case of Egypt. It is no secret that a competitive area for agricultural products between the United States and the European community has been the Egyptian market. This rivalry has resulted in a reduction of world market prices, which was of course aggravated by the fall of the dollar; the dollar is a reference currency and an account currency for most agricultural products.

Incontestably, Europe has benefited from this situation. But, so have countries such as Japan and the USSR, which also profit from a fall in the world market. There could have been a different outcome, an agreement between the European Common Market and the United States to agree to help Egypt solve its food security problem without forcing the world market of agricultural products to collapse. The paradox here is that in spite of the fall of the world wheat market, Egypt is obliged to subsidize bread production while the price of bread in Egypt is the lowest in the entire world! It is even lower than the world price per kilo of its own raw materials.

In conclusion, France has become one with Europe and has now accepted the loss of its own identity so that Europe as a whole may profit. This is how it is seen in the eyes of the Third World. In the future, France will no longer have a special policy towards the Third World except through its European partners. In my opinion, only Europe as a whole can respond to the challenge posed by the Third World, given the depth of its problems and needs.

DIALOGUE

QUESTION: You spoke briefly about the wheat war. In fact, it is even a more intensive issue, I believe. It has to do with the overproduction in developed countries and the rise in food production in traditionally friendly countries. In reality, the wheat war concerns all grains, and even meat-related products because of progress in the food industry. Productivity has multiplied two to three times. Are we moving towards an agreement to reduce food production?

VILGRAIN: I think one of the phenomena we experience is that almost everywhere in the world, except for a few Communist countries, there is food self-sufficiency. The only countries not able to solve their agricultural problems are the Communist countries, which are importing now. However, I believe, there is a general "de-Marxification" in agriculture. China and India, which for a time had communal planning in agriculture, are self-sufficient today. Thus, the only country that may remain an importer is the USSR because it is still a bastion of agricultural communism. In Africa, you have such problems as drought and other natural causes, which are not structural. On the contrary, countries like Ethiopia, which were extremely Marxist, had been self-sufficient before this political evolution and no longer are. Thus they are now importing. Others reduced their imports, such as Nigeria, which recently forbade wheat imports because it considered its food bowl too Westernized, and, as a country, it was becoming less Africanized. Producing millet and other grains replaces, more or less, what had been imported. This is not a Marxist phenomenon, but a trade balance phenomenon following the fall in oil prices. Thus, what I would like to point out is that due to the political events that I have just spoken about, there is incontestably a reduced demand. At the same time, there is also a rise in supply.

There is also a second phenomenon: the split between defense problems and food security. Take Japan for example. For years it subsidized rice production because it believed that in case of war, food products had to be stocked. Japan depends on outside sources for 70 percent of its food supply, so it decided to stockpile rice. These stocks have a considerable weight especially because the price actually paid for the rice is four to five times higher than the world market price. Recently, Japanese Prime Minister Nakasone said that he would consider this a political problem because this pairing of food security and defense is no longer valid. Strategic food stocks have also been stored in West Germany by the United States government. These large stocks ensure, during a certain period of time, food security in case of war. This phenomenon seems to be disappearing today. We in France have security stockpiles that were financed by the military. These no longer exist because we realize that the availability of food products is no longer linked to defense measures.

If the rise in supply is partly connected to a decrease in demand, it is also the incontestable result of a rise in productivity. Even Saudi Arabia is exporting food products this year. It produced 1.5 million tons of wheat but consumes only around 600,000 tons, thus producing more than twice its needs.

This rise in supply is real, but there could be other uses than food for agricultural products. For example, Brazil decided some time ago that sugar production could be used to produce alcohol for automobiles. The cost of producing sugar in Brazil helps the country avoid importing petroleum. One could argue, "But in the end you could find petroleum at a lower price than the alcohol you produce!" This is not certain. If we were to reason from a Brazilian point of view, we would realize that the price in cruzados to produce alcohol is not more expensive for the balance of trade than importing oil.

Therefore, I believe that the excess in supply in relation to food needs is a reality. However, today there are industrial uses for food. Starch, for example, has numerous other uses beyond nourishment. The United States is the primary world producer of starch, sending it worldwide for the manufacture of tires, pharmaceutical products, paper, etc.; products that today are becoming competitive due to the drop in agricultural prices.

The second element parallel to this fall in agricultural prices is a fall in the price of land. Some European industrialists now wonder if it would not be more profitable to invest in land rather than in industrial processes. In this way they could produce, under extremely competitive conditions, products that today have a guaranteed price in the European market due to a system of guaranteed agricultural revenues. But in the future, out of this context and completely integrated into another channel, such products could attain a stable return and could justify being substituted for petroleum or other similar products. The advent of biotechnologies is an interesting possibility.

QUESTION: What are the implications for company managers, like yourself, who earn their living in areas affected by the European Economic Community? If I take out my calendar, I have appointments as an American businessman. If you take out your calendar, these will be different because you are in an industry strongly influenced by political forces. How do you lead an administrative life that is so different and very much involved in international factors?

VILGRAIN: I think this is a very good question because the majority of managers in agro-industries in Europe visit the offices of European Community members as often as they visit their customers. I believe that the EEC agricultural situation is eminently a political one. Thus, the difference between your agenda and mine. You, when you see high-ranking civil servants, think about agricultural policies and the political issues that these policies raise. As for myself, I would say I actually live the consequences. If the political situation shifts, and if European budget problems, which are the key problems at this time, are not solved, European and American industries would be affected. For example, exactly one month ago, just by establishing a certain duty on so-called substitution products, the bottom fell out of the entire American starch industry.

Thus, just as an American industrialist does some lobbying in Washington, a European industrialist is obliged to do a little lobbying also in Brussels. This no longer takes place in Paris.

QUESTION: European political policy and the problems dealing with compensatory payments favor establishing companies in all European countries to limit the effect of the monetary compensatory amounts or to use them to benefit an industry. Is this the policy of your company?

VILGRAIN: No, our policy is not to take advantage of, but to avoid, the negative consequences due to the monetary compensatory amounts. I think no one knows how to take advantage of these amounts because they are more of a handicap than anything else. A number of German industrialists have succeeded in making some profit, but this was not due to any particular modification in their industrial strategy but to monetary changes. In general, investments in the agricultural food industry are quite heavy and cannot be managed and administered in two or three years. However, the evolution of monetary compensatory amounts can be decided in six months to a year and even less time. Therefore, this evolution has no effect on the industrial, commercial, or financial strategy of a group. Strategy is developed aside from any consideration of the compensatory payments. Nevertheless, a company's balance sheet can change fundamentally from one year to another depending on which side of the Rhine or the Channel the company is on. This is a function of monetary problems that are, in turn, a result of the rather erratic capital movement. The last meeting of the finance ministers in Paris may have somewhat regulated these movements because there seems to be a certain stability. Yet, these various capital shifts can be so large that an industrial strategy cannot be based on them. Of course, we are very much obliged to take them into account, when investing in dollars, Deutschemarks, or yen, but this is not fundamentally a primary motivation.

QUESTION: I find it surprising that large manufacturers do not consult with each other more often on a European level. It would seem easier to do this between industrial partners than with politicians.

VILGRAIN: European politics, in its plurality, is the European Parliament. This Parliament has one single function: to vote the budget. It is a large budget because it represents 1.4 percent of the value-added tax levied from the entire Community. Yet, those who have the power of decision in the Community are the members of the Commission, not politicians. They are people who have been named by politicians and have been influenced by political movements and who form a sort of administrative superstructure. They may be somewhat political, but they are most of all technocrats. They can be made to see that a certain decision will lead to certain consequences, serious or not. It is on this point, perhaps, that our agendas differ. We can attract their attention on certain technical issues. For example, we can show them that a particular approach or a type of aid will distort competition within the Community or internationally. American-type lobbying directed toward political representatives is not yet part of the European political system. This is simply because European political power is not strong enough.

QUESTION: It has often been claimed that Europe risks sinking under the weight of its agricultural policy, budget, and other problems. If you were responsible in Brussels for agriculture, what would be your policy to reconcile the agricultural interests on one hand and the general wider interests of Europe on the other?

VILGRAIN: This is a vast question. I cannot claim to have an answer. As a response, I am simply going to ask several questions. European defense policy has always been associated with agricultural policy. The pairing of the agricultural policy and European defense has been extremely important for twenty years, maybe because, historically, offensive attacks always occurred in the spring! Whatever the reason, for a long time food security has been such an important point that a journalist from the newspaper *Constellation* defined the latest weapon as the silo: to stockpile grain. In fact, since manufacturing nuclear weapons implies burning harvests, it became evident that any country that did not possess at least one year of stocked grains in advance had a great nuclear vulnerability because without such a reserve the country could not survive. This has been American policy for a very long time. Without such a reserve a country could not support nuclear deterrence. This was one of the important elements in President Carter's decision to put an embargo on wheat. In fact, one of the fragile points of the USSR's nuclear policy has been its agricultural problem; the country has had no food security. Not only because the northern ports are inaccessible because of the ice, but because the only supply points were Vladivostok or the North Sea. These are two extremely sensitive areas controlled by a relatively small marine contingency. Thus, the problem of food security concerns the East as well as the West.

Today there seems to be an uncoupling of these issues because we think of defense in a different light, and because overstocking is decreasing. Both in Europe and the United States stockpiling is simply on a one-year-in-advance basis. We no longer reach the levels known in 1955 or 1956 when the United States stocked three years ahead. It was a necessity then and was part of agro-power, as it was called at the time.

Thus, the first question is: Can our policies really separate defense problems from agricultural problems? I do not know. I believe that the defense debates we are currently having both in Europe and the United States also imply the same reasoning and perhaps a change. It was one of the most important points in defining the agricultural policy by France and its partners, when deciding a common agricultural policy for Europe.

The second question is one of income. When Europe elaborated its common agricultural policy, it definitely stopped agricultural migration to the cities, towards secondary or tertiary employment. Parallel to this, as a result or a residue of colonial policy, a large wave of labor flowed in to fill the needs of industry. Today, changing agricultural policy, thus reducing incomes, poses the problem of how to maintain this population in a rural setting where it will no longer have an income. It would also be necessary to find jobs in industry that were lost in agriculture. The percentage of the European population, including the Netherlands, in agriculture is higher than in the United States. Thus, I would say that any policy that blocks farmers' income implies a population transfer from agriculture to industry, or the tertiary services. This migration also runs up against the large number of Turkish, Algerian, and Tunisian immigrants all over Europe. These immigrants, at some point, became a substitute for agricultural migration.

It is on this point that we come back to the political problems with the Third World. What is to be done with this immigration population? You have lived through the same problems in the United States. There was the point in history marked by the *Grapes of Wrath* and the Mexican migration. Currently, Mexican agricultural workers are flowing back to Mexico. Some do stay, but they seek different kinds of employment, which will raise other issues. Europe has basically the same problem with its agricultural and immigration population.

How will this be resolved? It is a difficult European political decision. Will the Germans agree in relation to the Turkish population, the French in relation to the Algerians or the Tunisians, or the English with the Pakistanis and the immigrants from Hong Kong? I do not know. It is each country's problem, but it is also Europe's problem.

QUESTION: Taking into account the current price of oil, is transforming agricultural products profitable?

VILGRAIN: That is always the problem. I have often had discussions with American friends in my profession who believe it is profitable. My question to them is: "At what price are you placing the dollar?" I shall remind you that one and a half years ago when the dollar was at eleven francs, Europe needed no subsidies in order to export in the world market. But production costs of American agriculture were also at eleven francs because its selling price was eleven francs. Today the dollar is at six francs, but production costs have not changed in United States or Europe. So it all depends. It is difficult to speak in terms of production costs and say it is more profitable in one place or the other. It all depends on which currency you are dealing in and at what level that currency happens to be.

QUESTION: France has always been more closely linked to Maghrebin countries than have other members of the Common Market. Do you think in the future France will be able to reconcile its European role with its obligations toward its former colonies?

VILGRAIN: Until recently, France, along with Italy, was the only country bordering the Mediterranean to define its European policy in this area. Now there are two other countries, Greece and Spain. Thus, France's Mediterranean policy that was for a time bilateral between France and Italy has now become quadrilateral. Without a doubt, both Greece and Spain have a voice in the European entity and can block any number of measures. This means that France cannot have a policy in the Mediterranean area very different from that of its other Common Market partners. I shall give the example of olive oil because that is what everyone is talking about now. The prime minister has heightened the sensitivity of public opinion in this matter and it has become a stone in the European garden. Olive oil can be produced in Europe, in Spain, Greece, and

Italy, or it can be produced in Tunisia. If it is produced on both sides we come back to the point that there will be a huge excess in supply. This would also affect sunflower oil production and the importation of soybeans from the United States. It is all together. Everything is linked in these agricultural food products; one can substitute for the other. You cannot reason away the olive oil problem by simply saying we will eliminate olives. The problem goes beyond this. It is a Mediterranean problem. Unfortunately, this is the kind of problem the Common Market is entangled in. Today it is this particular problem; tomorrow it will be another one that needs to be solved. There is a will to formulate policies that favor collaboration on both sides of the Mediterranean, yet we confront specific problems like these.

PART II

A Business Revolution?

I

Economic Policy

Serge Bellanger
Olivier Blanchard

BELLANGER

We all live in an unstable economic world: budget and trade deficits, unemployment, imbalances in financial resources between developed and developing countries, trade disputes with their underlying risk of protectionism, and the instability of exchange rates. These are some of the fundamental issues that affect the course of national economies. Many countries have their ups and downs, and their paths may shift or alternate from time to time. Such is the case with my country, France.

An article recently published in a French newspaper concluded that there was a correlation between the state of the French economy and the laughter of the French people. According to this analysis, in 1939, people used to laugh for an average of nineteen minutes a day. It declined to six minutes a day in 1980, and to one minute a day in 1984. These statistics are scary, especially when we know that one minute of laughter is equivalent to forty-five minutes of exercise, according to a French doctor!

Before I discuss the new liberal route that has recently emerged as the path of the future as well as the privatization program that will drastically modify our economic landscape, I shall make some preliminary statements.

The first concerns language. Words and phrases like *liberalism, pragmatism, liberal democracy, conservatism,* and *free market policy* can of course be translated into many foreign languages but in most cases may have different meanings. This is certainly true for France.

The second is the role of the state in any economy. This has been a controversial topic for more than a decade and will continue to generate debate in the future for politicians, businessmen, and scholars. There is no universal answer to such complex questions as: Is there a need for some form of industrial policy? If yes, what should be its extent? What is a regulated economy? What should a government do or not do? Each country formulates its own policy based on its history, traditions, and its social and economic environment. But too often people look upon differences between two societies with the perception of their own value systems.

In France, ideology has dominated politics for a long time, whereas in the United States, for example, politicians are more pragmatic and more receptive to business concerns than their counterparts abroad. However, this situation is rapidly changing in France and elsewhere. It is only recently that a new generation of French politicians has become more pragmatic in the formulation of policies. A new liberal economy for France means that the role of the government should be progressively curtailed and that economic agents should be liberated from some bureaucratic constraints and state intervention. The government wants to inject more freedom into the economic and social systems, to put an end to state interventionism, and to promote individual initiative.

This is the basic philosophy of the current administration meant to advance our society, and it is a major revolution for the French mentality. But, as in any business venture, to define a policy is one thing; to implement it is another, and at this juncture, the challenge for the Chirac administration is on the latter front.

Liberalism has emerged as a trend for the future of France under the pressure of three major forces:

1. With economic globalization and technological development, France has to open up its economy in order to respond to the growing international economic competition on the one side, and to the challenge of a truly European economy by 1992 on the other. After all, France is the fourth or fifth economic power in the world behind the United States, Japan, and Germany.

2. The second force is political, and the consequence of two alternating shifts in power in five years. When the Socialists took over in 1981, they implemented a highly centralized economic program which increased the role of the state. But under the pressure of market realities, this leftist coalition became social-democratic, and in 1985 started to move toward a more liberal path. Various measures were taken including a progressive deregulation of financial markets.

   Today we are experiencing what we call "cohabitation," which is well accepted in this country (According to a recent survey, more than 65 percent of American citizens are in favor of this concept for the United States) but has not yet been tested in France, for the very simple reason that French institutions were not set up for this type of dual leadership. Indeed, it has worked better than most people originally thought at the beginning—at least through October 1986. But clouds have appeared over the past several months. A Sofres-LePoint survey of February 10 shows that only 45 percent of the French people are pleased with this power sharing, versus 71 percent in October and 66 percent in December. Prime Minister Chirac cannot do everything he wants in order to end decades of state interventionism.

Demonstrations by students and the strikes in the transportation sector in December 1986 were not attacks on the division of powers between the president and the prime minister as some may have implied. Rather, they confirm that the passage of a bill is not sufficient to transform a society. More is needed: dialogue and working together with labor forces and consumer groups, and it is generally recognized today that the lesson has been understood.

3. Finally, the level of education of the young, the progressive change in habits and in perception of values, as well as social progress have led the French to observe that the most successful and powerful countries are those that are liberal.

LIBERALISM: A PRAGMATIC APPROACH

Socialists in 1981 implemented an expansionary economic program based on ideology and the belief that banks were wealthy (the "wall of money" metaphor often raised by the Left) and had hidden reserves, and that corporations had profit-oriented strategies that did not promote the social objectives of the state. The cornerstone of the Socialist program was, of course, the nationalization of nine major industrial groups and thirty-six banks and financial institutions. Although the state poured money into these nationalized firms, much of it went to cover massive losses in 1982–1983. And as the 1986 elections approached, Socialists were hampered by the fact that efforts to undo their early damage to the economy were not succeeding.

They subsequently reassessed their economic policy and allowed corporations to pursue their own markets rather than asking them to conform to some constraining or ill-defined public purpose. The Socialists finally realized that the allocation of national wealth has nothing to do with the techniques that produce that wealth. But it was acknowledged that the Socialists bore the tremendous burden of economic mistakes and ultimately lost the legislative elections in March 1986.

The common platform of the Center-Right opposition in January 1986 favored both the liberalization of the economy through a program of deregulation that is expected to stimulate market forces and liberate firms from state constraints and the denationalization of banks and corporations that had been nationalized after 1981.

The government led by Jacques Chirac did not try, as the Socialists did, to maintain an ideological approach. Rather, it decided to recognize potential constraints and obstacles, such as the weight of old traditions and the dominance of the state, and to follow a pragmatic and moderate route. But if it has been successful on some fronts (e.g., privatizations), it has failed on others (reform of universities and merit salary increases at the SNCF, for example). France is indeed a very conservative country, and despite the fact that the common thinking is moving in the direction of liberalism, French society is still very rigid; many French people are strong advocates of deeply rooted traditions based on centuries of history.

CONTROL BY THE STATE

The basic problem of French society is the complexity of the decision-making process among nationalized corporations, collectivities, the administration, and the government. Resistance to change is entrenched in three areas.

First, France is still heavily controlled by the state and has been historically a highly centralized society. Bureaucracy is very constraining, and since the seventeenth century all politicians—conservative and leftists alike—have developed the government's control and support of industry and promoted *dirigisme*.

Second, on social grounds, protectionism, state assistance, and the permanent fight for safeguarding or maintaining acquired rights and privileges remain. This is also true for labor organizations, employers' associations, and the government. As a result, our society is more preoccupied with the reanimating of fights dating back to the Industrial Revolution than with economic realities such as the competitiveness of our industry or labor relations. Our economy has lost ground nationally and internationally.

Finally, the state is the first shareholder, the first employer, the first manufacturer, and the only bank, with 90 percent of total deposits. Therefore, the French economic system lacks flexibility, does not promote individual initiative, and is not sufficiently market oriented. Relationships between corporations and the state are highly complex. And yet, France has vast resources in many fields such as high technology, biochemistry, engineering, and aerospace, but we do not always know how to go from the research laboratory to the plant and from the plant to the marketplace—the so-called marketing gap. For example, after nationalization, some 30 percent of all industrial sales and 24 percent of French employees were controlled by the public sector; the state also controlled 85 percent of all credit allocations.

Between 1982 and July 1984, the cost of nationalized companies for the state has been estimated at FF 178 billion. Accumulated losses amounted to FF 20 billion in 1982 and FF 16.5 billion in 1983, although most of the public sector returned to the black by 1984. But earnings are not yet sufficient to sustain growth and to respond to the challenge of foreign competition. State involvement has become unbearable not only for government but for private competition, business leaders, and labor forces. A continuation of this policy would be detrimental to the future of corporations and would rapidly jeopardize the national economy.

According to a recent survey, 63 percent of French people support a liberalized economic program, but they want to be part of the decision-making process rather than being asked to accept unilaterally new rules of the game. The writer

Guy Sorman once said, "Liberalism is a simple idea which works." He might be right, but recent events seem to indicate that liberalism is an idea that works when it is simple. But France is not unique. Many countries are reassessing the state's role in the business sector; it is therefore not surprising that privatization has become a worldwide trend in the 1980s, which most governments are either already pursuing or actively considering.

THE NEW LIBERAL ECONOMY

The Chirac administration has had major accomplishments in a relatively short period of time. The government has three basic objectives: (1) to adjust the course of the economy and to improve its efficiency, (2) to bring greater flexibility and more freedom into the economic and social systems, and (3) to promote popular capitalism.

On one level, monetary adjustments were made in 1986. External debt was reduced from FF 41 billion to FF 7 billion, and the budget deficit was cut down to FF 144 billion from FF 159 billion through a reduction program of public spending (2.5 percent of GNP versus 3 percent in 1985). On another level, price control mechanisms dating back to 1945 have been removed, and it is believed that this is an irreversible trend. Ninety percent of foreign exchange controls have been eliminated; a more efficient credit control system based on open-market policy and interest rates has replaced the rigid quantitative control of credit implemented after the Second World War; an antitrust commission (*Commission de la Concurrence*) has been created; and the financial market is currently being renovated. And the privatization program, the cornerstone of this liberal program, on which I will now elaborate, is progressing successfully.

PRIVATIZATION: A WORLDWIDE TREND

A number of factors justify privatization. To begin with, budget deficits resulting from slow economic growth, rising unemployment, and social expenditures have led many countries (including the United States) to sell or liquidate assets rather than to increase taxes. Also, government's inefficient running of industrial corporations has led to the growing realization that private management is more cost-effective and market-oriented. In addition, the recent development of financial and equity markets as well as a better understanding of basic economic principles by a growing number of employees is helping to privatize state-owned enterprises. Finally, the internationalization of capital markets allows the base of stockholders to be broadened and markets abroad to be explored.

Among industrial countries, the United Kingdom and France have two of the largest privatization programs, but Italy, Spain, and Austria also have programs to sell assets. Other countries are actively considering privatization with various degrees of bureaucratic and ideological resistance, including Chile, Brazil, Mexico, Argentina, India, Turkey, and Nigeria.

THE FRENCH PRIVATIZATION PROGRAM

In July 1986, the French legislature passed a law providing that majority interests owned directly or indirectly in sixty-five companies (forty-five nationalized in 1982 and twenty nationalized in 1945) would be transferred to the private sector no later than March 1, 1991. This extensive plan for selling off state enterprises on the stock market, estimated at FF 330 billion or $47 billion in January 1986, does not appear unrealistic. It represents approximately one-third of the current capitalization of the French market, about FF 900 billion, with a daily turnover of FF 1 billion. In the long term, this program should help increase significantly the size and depth of the French stock market and improve its position among European markets (The New York market accounts for 50 percent of worldwide capitalization, Japan 25 percent, and Europe 25 percent).

The law has also instituted a complex procedure requiring that a Privatization Commission value corporations and publish its findings. The method of distribution—sale of shares, exchange of shares for subordinated preferred shares (*titres participatifs*) or nonvoting common shares (*certificats d'investissement*), etc.—is decided by the Ministry of Finance. Ten percent are available as discount shares for employees, up to 30 percent may be sold through private placements, and the remaining 60 percent sold on the stock market. The Ministry of Finance must approve any holding exceeding 10 percent of the company's capital by one individual or a group of individuals acting in concert, and foreigners can buy up to 20 percent of the total shares.

The first company to be privatized, in December 1986, was Saint-Gobain, a profitable diversified industrial group. The privatization was a major success, and Saint-Gobain now has more than 1.5 million shareholders. The second company to be denationalized, in February 1987, was Paribas, the fifth-largest French banking group. To achieve its objective, Paribas developed an active public relations campaign, and the capital, which had been oversubscribed 2.5 times, was distributed among 3.5 million shareholders. The third company to be denationalized, during the second quarter of 1987, is Compagnie Générale d'Electricite (CGE), which recently signed an important joint venture agreement with the ITT Corporation in the telecommunications sector. Other companies considered for the next wave of privatization are Agence Havas (a major advertising firm), Société Générale (one of the three leading banks that were nationalized in 1945), TF1 (television), and some banks (Crédit Commercial de France and others).

The market capitalization of shares has risen from 9 percent of France's GNP in 1978 to 13 percent in 1985 and to some 25 percent today, compared to 25 percent in Germany, 52 percent in the United States, and 80 percent in the United Kingdom. This success, however, should not hide potential concerns. A key issue is not simply going from the governmental sector to the private sector but ensuring that corporations with the same management can be more successful than in the past and contribute to the growth of national output.

Some experts have called the first two denationalizations a "governmental privatization" since the sale did not bring additional capital to the newly privatized companies. It is anticipated that in the future a capital increase will be associated with the denationalization process. Another area that deserves close watch is the changing attitudes and behaviors of senior management, employees, and labor forces as well as the new relationship with boards of directors, which should be more involved in strategic planning and decision making and more sensitive to the corporation's performance and profitability. Other issues, such as the liquidity of the stock market, also cannot be ignored.

Privatization is a major component of the economic program of the Chirac administration. It should be a major success and help the government to achieve its three main objectives: improve the efficiency of the economy, liberate businessmen from bureaucratic constraints, and pave the way for a more liberal society through dynamic policies.

A FIRST-YEAR BALANCE SHEET

The economic performance in 1986 was good: Real economic activity rose from 1 percent in 1985 to 2 percent in 1986; investments increased by 4 percent (16 percent for middle-sized companies with fewer than one hundred employees against a negative growth in 1985); 50,000 jobs were created; and inflation was cut by 50 percent from 4.7 percent in 1985 to 2.1 percent in 1986. The situation of our trade balance, however, remains weak. It still reflects French companies' lack of competitiveness in foreign markets.

On the other hand, 1987 might be difficult. Our trade deficit in January (1987) was FF 2.5 billion, partly due to the increase in oil prices and the December strikes; our unemployment rate increased by 1.5 percent; and the price index was 0.8 percent for the month of January, which partially reflected the change from a state-controlled economy to a liberal economic system.

Changes in attitudes and the behavior of economic agents are encouraging, although natural resistance to modifications still exists. It is on this ground that the government will face its main challenge. Social and political forces cannot be underestimated. This is true everywhere but it is even more true in France. The government has not much leeway in the current political environment where all party leaders have their eyes directed towards the 1988 presidential horizon, and it cannot afford to make the same mistakes the Socialists did in 1982. Pragmatism and cooperation have to prevail over ideology.

It is fair to say that the Socialists, by initiating neoliberalism and deregulation during their last years of power, have helped to promote a new spirit of change. Liberalism is likely to be irreversible, although some indicate that France is no more liberal today than it was socialist in 1981.

The challenge for France is to reach a balance between an old civilization deeply rooted in history and a modern and efficient economic and social system in order to share the leadership of this world with other major industrialized nations. We have the human and technological resources, and we now have the political wits to change our society and its basic structure to adjust to the new parameters of a world economy. A pragmatic, progressive, and liberal route can be successful for France and help its economy to grow and to close the gap with our major trading partners, particularly West Germany and the United States. The fundamental question, "Liberalism: too much or not enough" will probably be assessed carefully by the Chirac administration throughout 1987 both in economic and political terms.

BLANCHARD

I am not as optimistic as Mr. Bellanger. What can we expect from French macroeconomic policy, as opposed to microeconomic policy, and the French economy to do over the next two to five years? The answer is, not much. Let me explain why I think that.

The way to understand where we are today requires us to go back to the beginning of the 1980s in Europe and the United States. There was the general feeling around 1980 that something was very wrong with the way economies were working, that the state was playing much too important a role in economic life, that inflation and unemployment were both too high, and that these factors were closely interrelated. As a result, there was a wave of conservative policies, but the directions these policies took were quite different in the United States and Europe.

In the United States, the political bet was that to reduce the size of the government, the first step was to reduce taxes, create big deficits, apply pressure, and hope that spending would go down. It may well work—we don't know yet. In Europe the policy was quite different. The first thing the government should do, it was widely agreed, was to put its financial house in order, namely reduce deficits, shrink in size, return to balanced budgets, tighten the money supply to reduce inflation, and put pressure on real wages and make firms more competitive. The two countries taking the lead in this direction at the beginning of the 1980s were the United Kingdom under Margaret Thatcher and Germany; they have remained in the lead ever since. Our country, however, decided for a while to go its own way, having a different diagnosis. Socialist France thought that a way out of economic difficulty was to expand, to try to grow out of its problems. This approach turned out not to work; France got trade deficits, successive devaluations and, very soon thereafter, its macroeconomic policy was more or less indistinguishable from that of Germany and the United Kingdom.

The point here is that macroeconomic policies, not the reorganization of the private sector or the role of the government, are what distinguished France from Germany and the United Kingdom. These policies were implemented starting at slightly different times in both countries (around 1979 in the United Kingdom and about 1982 in Germany); they were introduced in France in 1983. We can now more or less assess how they have worked. In my opinion, the results were mixed. The role of the government, measured by the size of the government in economic activity, has been slightly reduced, but not very much. Looking at the numbers very closely, you see reductions of 1 percent or 2 percent of the gross national product at most. Not much therefore, although perhaps the composition of government's role has changed more drastically. In terms of inflation, there has been, to a very large extent, success. Inflation is low in Germany; it is close to being negative in the United Kingdom. In France it is surprisingly lower than anybody would have expected a year ago. We had a bit of help along the way from the foreign oil prices, but in large part it was due to the fiscal and monetary contraction.

The macroeconomic policies have failed, however, on the growth and the unemployment fronts. One of the reasons these policies were initiated in 1980 was the feeling that unemployment was too high. It is now on average twice as high as it was in 1980. The degree to which it has increased and decreased varies by country, Germany having had a smaller increase, for example, than France or the United Kingdom; overall, however, we now have very high levels of unemployment, and it is not decreasing if you look at Europe as a whole. In fact, it actually increased by a few tenths of a percent in the last year.

Nobody expected this slowdown in growth and this very high persistence in unemployment. We can conservatively predict at this stage that if we keep applying the same set of policies as have been applied in the last five years, the economies will not return to full employment by themselves, as they had hoped in 1983, 1984, 1985, and 1986. Predictions from either the OECD or EEC always implied that we would slowly go back to "normal," and every year the forecast is revised downwards. Things are improving but, at best, at a very slow rate. The question is what is needed now, because we cannot stay with an average of 10 percent unemployment in Europe or 11 percent in France.

What is needed is a combination of policies or what can be called a two-handed approach—the use of both supply measures and demand measures. Supply measures may mean denationalization, shrewd denationalization, more flexibility of firms to hire and to fire people, and policies that lower labor and other costs. But by itself, this approach is far from enough. What is also needed is the assurance for France that even with these lower costs it can actually sell more to both the internal market in Europe and elsewhere in the world. There must be confidence that the market is growing. Hence, a combination of supply and demand policies is required. Pure supply policies just do not work by themselves. Further, they are very hard to implement.

I think the 1986 French student riots are a very good example of the problems that arise when you try to attack problems on the supply side without doing anything on the demand side. Let me explain. The French university system is clearly not in good shape. There is no question that there should be more competition of some sort in the university system, but there also should be more selection. The university system cannot simply be a way of avoiding teenage unemployment, which is, to a large extent, what it is. There is no question that there should be more selection. However, the students at this stage have a very low probability of getting a job if they cannot go to the university. It is not difficult to understand their reaction. When you know that the alternative to going to the university is becoming unemployed, you are going to fight very hard to keep the right to go to the university. If things had been different, that is, if those who were not able to go to the university could have gotten jobs in the private sector, my impression is that the student riots of 1986 might still have occurred because student uprisings are part of French tradition, but they would have had a milder political impact. The lesson is clear: If you can provide the jobs then you can actually ask people to accept more flexibility, for example, in firing and hiring or in education. You can introduce more selection, but you cannot keep asking workers to give up protection, to give up tenure, if forfeiting tenure means a good probability of being permanently unemployed when fired. You need both supply and demand measures. And I think that has not yet been fully understood by all people in government in various European countries.

Now if this diagnosis is correct, what should or can France do? This is where I'm fairly pessimistic. France is a small country in Europe; it is a small country in the world, and it is only part of Europe. To the extent that other countries are not ready to embark on such policies, it is very difficult for a single country in Europe to go it alone. We have one attempt in that—the French socialist experiment. This was bungled in many ways, but at least there was the idea that perhaps a long recession was not needed to cure many structural and economic ills. The Socialists in power believe that we could have more growth than the others. The result was that as we expanded our economies, and others did not, we generated a very large trade deficit. The combination of a trade deficit and the fact that the government was socialist created speculation on the franc, devaluations, and forced us to stop. It is my impression that even if the current government were to embark on a similar policy, it would surely run into the same problems: It would run into a trade deficit. If you try to push things faster than your neighbors you get deficits, as for example, has the United States, although the United States can survive them. So, this is the first problem for any country that wants to go it alone. And this is why in general I'm not very optimistic: I do not see the degree of coordination among Germany, the United Kingdom, and France that will avoid that problem. This is the first reason for pessimism.

The second reason for pessimism, which is relevant for the short term, is that when tough policies are needed, probably the worst political system you can have is cohabitation. I think that any good set of policies at this stage implies that for a while the government will have to be unpopular. It will have to run risks. It will have to run the risk of a trade deficit. It will have to run the risk of inflation. It will run the risk that the policy does not work. But with cohabitation, any government that tries to implement a given economic policy can be fired the minute its popularity goes down. This is very much how the system works. If Prime Minister Chirac were to take strong decisions, with a strong program, and the results of the first six months were dismal (which is not an unlikely outcome), he would not be there after six months. There would just be no way of obtaining the fruits of that policy. Thus cohabitation also prevents Prime Minister Chirac from doing anything grandiose, ambitious, or risky. My impression is, therefore, that until the next elections, nothing is going to happen on the macroeconomic front. Demand is not going to be stimulated very much. There is going to be some improvement on the supply side, but I do not see much further growth or more ambitious policies. After the elections, cohabitation may end, but then the problem of coordination will face European countries. When Germany moves there will be room for more optimism.

DIALOGUE

MODERATOR: Based on the two preceding points of view, we have a general sense that a lot has changed. The rhetoric of socialism has been replaced by the rhetoric of capitalism. It's very surprising for Americans to see. French high school students are now swarming to get a high school diploma in math, instead of Latin and Greek as in the past, and flooding in to get MBAs instead of becoming *agrégés*. French people are rushing to buy shares of stock when companies are being privatized. These are things that we never would have expected five or ten years ago in France. So a lot has changed. But on the other hand, the economic results haven't changed so much. There seems to be a continuity of the trends in the last ten years, regardless of the government in power. Other things beyond the change of people and political administrations are responsible for the lack of change in French society. And I would say that it's largely a result of insufficient change, incorrect change; change of rhetoric isn't enough, change of people isn't enough; economic rigidities remain in French society. These political decisionmaking and social rigidities are leading to the poor economic performance of France.

QUESTION: How does French economic performance compare to that of other European countries?

BELLANGER: It is true that the problem of France has to be looked at in the European context. If we compare Blanchard's figures for the 1981 situation to those of Germany, for example, we see that the French economy and the German economy were practically on the same footing. We are converging more and more with the Germans. It seems to me that politically we have made mistakes, but I think we are now closer to the German economy because European integration has to be based on France and Germany.

BLANCHARD: Yes, I agree with what you've said. At the same time I think one should not overemphasize the difference between Germany and France. I think the vision that many people have of Germany doing well and France doing poorly is not correct. Germany is not doing well. Germany is doing roughly the same except that it has slightly lower unemployment. In terms of growth, the results are very similar. In terms of investment, France is right in the middle of the European pack. It is actually doing slightly better than the pack for 1986 and is expected to do better in 1987. It is very clear that there is a set of European problems that are the dominant source of problems, and then there are additional specific French problems.

QUESTION: Mr. Blanchard, how reliable are the unemployment figures given the existence of an extensive cash economy in some European countries? I know, for instance, that the Italians have a 13.9 percent rate of unemployment but the cash economy is rumored to account for something like 25–30 percent of the national income. What is your feeling about the reliability of unemployment figures?

BLANCHARD: This is a hard question to answer precisely, because the numbers are not recorded and that's why we have to guess. I think there are two things to be said. First, if you had been told five years ago that European countries would have between 8–18 percent unemployment, which is roughly the range from France to Spain, and have no major political upheavals as a result of it, you would have been very surprised. The only way to explain why we haven't had any is that unemployment isn't as costly for those who are unemployed as it was twenty or thirty years ago; few of the unemployed are starving. In that sense, maybe unemployment is not as painful as the pure numbers suggest.

Of the actual number of people defined as unemployed, some are working either part time or on the side. There have been only a few studies of this question. In Spain, with close to 20 percent unemployed, a study was done that showed that maybe 2–3 percent of the 20 percent unemployed people were working on the side, undeclared; this still leaves 17 percent. There are fascinating statistics for the Netherlands about the number of people on legal disability. These are people legally disabled and therefore paid but not working. The number ten years ago was 2 percent of the labor force, according to economists, a standard number of people who have a functional disability. The number last year was 13 percent. The increase was mostly due to psychological disabilities, which are slightly more difficult to verify. So if you add the official unemployment number, which I think is around 13 percent or 14 percent now, to what must be something like 10 percent, you actually get a staggering number: Probably 25 percent of the labor force which is not working.

QUESTION: With respect to entrepreneurship and innovation, it is my understanding that in France the leader of an unsuccessful business venture is barred by law from either starting or heading another enterprise. If my understanding is correct, this contrasts markedly with experience in the United States where successful enterprises are very often started by people who have as many as two or more unsuccessful ventures. Are there any emerging changes in the law or business culture that indicate a greater willingness to accept a small percentage of failures for a larger return of success?

BELLANGER: There is a distinction in the French legislation between voluntary bankruptcy and involuntary bankruptcy, and if one takes the initiative to apply to the courts, as you do in your Chapter 11, there is no taint on one's future career. However, if the indebtedness is so colossal that one is brought to bankruptcy by one's creditors, then that taint does preclude him from starting up another commercial venture in his name in a managerial capacity.

QUESTION: I have a question about managerial flexibility and ability to lay off employees. What changes have occurred? What changes do you think are needed to increase employment in France?

MODERATOR: Managers now have the ability to reduce employment or to lay off employees for economic reasons. But let's not forget that the administrative controls on layoffs were put in place under Giscard when Chirac was prime minister the first time. Through a combination of negotiations with unions and decrees of the current minister of labor, companies are now freer to manage their employment levels. But this has not had the impact on unemployment that many doomsayers had anticipated. First, the state has not completely freed the hands of managers; in cases where there has been a strong public outcry against reduction of employment, the minister of labor or his labor inspectors have intervened. Second, in spite of complaining for many years about the restrictions, many managers hesitate, finding that they are unaccustomed to managing layoffs.

BELLANGER: It is difficult to know exactly who was fired as a result of loosening the restrictions on layoffs. When you go from a system that has fairly stringent restrictions on firing to a system that has less stringent restrictions, you go through a period of transition during which people are kept on by companies. Later on, the added flexibility reduces the average labor cost, allowing firms to be more entrepreneurial and take risks knowing that if something doesn't work they can reduce the labor force more easily.

QUESTION: Mitterrand was elected in 1981, enacting policies that everybody seems to agree were disastrous. The Socialists then enacted policies that seemed to have been good for business. What difference has socialism made?

BELLANGER: Well I think that assuming that in 1986 Chirac had not come to power, the Socialists would have privatized some corporations, because the shift in socialism was well on its way. I must say, by the way, that even back in 1985, some Socialists in power at the time thought we should do something to denationalize every company. It seems to me that when you look at the financial markets—financial markets have deteriorated—more was done under the Socialists than is being done today. So it seems to me that if Chirac had not been chosen prime minister, France would probably have followed the same type of liberal path.

QUESTION: There is one phenomenon that we didn't talk too much about which is the big decline of the Communist party. My question is how do you view this decline? Is it something like a temporary phenomenon or is it a real historical decline of the Communist party and union in France?

BELLANGER: I think this is a major, irreversible decline. The French Communist party and union have failed to adapt to a changing society. But trade unions are not dead. In periods of high unemployment traditionally what happens is the national unions do badly because they are thought not able to solve the national problems. Yet there is considerable unhappiness at the firm level; the fact that the national unions are weak doesn't mean that the workers are happy. Workers in France have accepted real wage cuts, or no real wage increases, in many sectors for many years now. I think that what has been said about the strikes at the end of last year are a symptom that although our national unions are weak, it doesn't mean there is not discontent at a much lower level, which could be a potential problem.

2

Investment Patterns and Practices

Jean-Paul Angé
Jean-François Carreras

ANGÉ

"Investment Patterns and Practices" is a very broad subject, which I will try to restrict to a few topics. The title of this session refers to the multiple financial decisions that take place between investors, companies, and other important operators like the government and public agencies. These transactions among borrowers, lenders, and operators occur in places designated collectively under the name of, obviously, *market*. What I propose to explore are the recent changes in the French financial market and the impact they have had on U.S. operators.

Although I was introduced as an expert in mergers and acquisitions, my expertise is strictly in international mergers and acquisitions. My principal involvement, since most of my clients are U.S. corporations, is handling their transactions in Western Europe, mostly in France.

Before I present a brief description of the Paris financial market, I would like to make two points. First, I would like to demolish the stereotype of the individual French investor being in love with only one commodity: gold. I would say that the stereotypical investor in France, who was supposed to stash gold coins in wool socks and hide them under his mattress, is an endangered though not extinct species. The second point I would like to make is that the French markets are not as much fun or spectacular as the U.S. markets. You would find it extremely difficult to find an individual in Paris able to pay a fine of $100 million as Mr.

Boesky did. It's not so much that the French are not greedy, it is just that they lack opportunities.

Another example of the dramatic side of the New York market appeared this morning in the *Financial Times*. The first page headline read: "New York Stock Exchange starts trading in insults." Apparently a dispute is developing between the New York and London stock exchanges because the New York Stock Exchange barred its members from trading in jointly listed securities during the hours when the New York Stock Exchange is open. The London representative said that the New York decision was antediluvian. The president of the New York Stock Exchange said that the London market did not really count as a stock exchange at all and then added, "If the London Stock Exchange wants to be what a stock exchange looks like, feels like, and smells like, that's their business." The Brits said, "Who wants to look like, feel like, and smell like something Neanderthal?" And so on. Unfortunately the French are not trading in insults yet, but if we open a market in that commodity, I'm sure we'll do very well.

Let's go back to the dry matter of financial markets in Paris. During the past forty years, financial markets in France, the money markets that include banking systems, have been characterized by an extreme degree of protection given the investor. One example: In twenty years, not a single French bank has gone bankrupt. As you know, in the United States, banks go bankrupt every year, half a dozen every month, small banks of course. Why has no French bank gone bankrupt? Not because they are better managed than any other bank in the world, but because there is a system of solidarity organized by the French Treasury Department that makes it very difficult for a bank to go bankrupt, even if it wants to.

Let me give you an overview of the regulatory bodies in France. First and foremost of course is the Direction du Trésor, whose U.S. counterpart is the Treasury Department. Second is the central bank, Banque de France, whose U.S. counterpart is the Federal Reserve. In the bond and stock market, there is the body called COB, Commission des Opérations de Bourse, equivalent to the SEC, and in the real estate financing area, there is a body, little known outside of France, called Crédit Foncier that does not really have an equivalent in the United States, even though some of its functions are assumed by government agencies.

Five years ago, the French markets were definitely unsophisticated. To achieve the degree of security and protection that I mentioned before, the market had been, by tradition and regulation, divided into various isolated submarkets. One is the monetary market, which is a market between the banks and the reserve bank. The real estate financing market is also isolated from the other markets, and the financial securities market is a third market. On top of that, there is no continuity between short- and long-term instruments and no way to refinance, to go back and forth between the two markets. So short term and long term were totally different. As a matter of fact, as an example, in France the Crédit National is the only lender from which a company can borrow money for more than ten years. While the Paris markets were remaining frozen in their ways, the Anglo-Saxon markets—New York, London, Hong Kong—were moving very actively towards a new financial array of products and markets through phenomena that have been called securitization and disintermediation. The French authorities came to the realization that they could not leave the Paris market outside of a worldwide trend that was making the walls crumble between all the various financial instruments and decided to gradually modernize the Paris financial markets.

A number of the creations on the equity side have resulted from this modernization. A new market has been created called the "Second Marché," the Second Market, which is more or less equivalent to the over-the-counter market in this country. It has been a tremendous success. In the short-term instruments area, *des certificats de dépot*, or CDs, have been created. Also in the area of short-term investments, *des billets de trésorerie*, very similar to the commercial paper in the United States have been issued.

New products, new bonds, have been put on the market, and, in essence, a new treasury market has been created in Paris renovating the antiquated operating practices of the French Treasury. Futures have been introduced on the Paris market, a *marché à terme d'instruments financiers* (MATIF) on which I think only two or three contracts are traded right now, but that should change. Another big move was to allow banks to negotiate their fees with brokers, a practice that has existed in this country for more than ten years. Soon an options market is going to be started.

This list is interesting in the sense that for every creation, every new instrument, every new market, there is an almost exact U.S. equivalent, a corresponding market or instrument. The reason is simple: The French Treasury decided to catch up to the world market by importing American concepts with few changes. This type of pragmatic attitude is not always typical in France, or elsewhere in the world, because people don't like to imitate, they prefer to reinvent. In this case, however, the approach has been very effective, albeit gradual. And, obviously, there is still a long way to go to make Paris, which in any case will never become a big world financial center, as modern and aggressive as London, a more logical comparison than New York because of its proximity.

From an American point of view, one of the most shocking aspects on the security side of the business is the fact that the Paris Bourse, the Paris stock exchange, is reserved to a closed number of brokers, *les agents de change*, who are individuals. Therefore, no seat can be bought by a firm, as is possible, even if it must be done indirectly, on the New York Stock Exchange. In Paris there is a limit, I think, of 143 brokers, and it's extremely difficult to move that monopoly. The result is that the brokerage firms are undercapitalized family businesses, which represent an obstacle to the modernization of the Paris Bourse. The fees are fixed except in the case of banks, which now have the right to negotiate them. However, there is a schedule of fees for the individual investor, and therefore there is no competition on the fees as there is in the United States with the discount brokerage houses.

To what degree are U.S. operators, investors, companies, etc., affected by these changes? There are 400 banks in Paris of which 142 are foreign banks, of which probably about a third are American, although I don't have the exact figure. Foreign banks represent 15 percent in total assets of all the French banks, 12 percent in lending, 8 percent in deposits. The low level of deposits is easy to understand since foreign banks in France do not engage in retail banking. Therefore they have to borrow on the market. At present, in the context of the modernization of the French financial markets, U.S. banks in Paris, in addition to executing the traditional banking functions of advising its clients, exporting letters of credits, and so on, are contributing their knowledge of the products, the instruments. These technologies have existed in this country for many years and are now being implemented in France.

Let me give you an example. Two or three years ago, a French law was passed allowing leveraged buy-outs. The French banks have been extremely reluctant to go into LMBOs or LBOs; the most aggressive lenders in Paris now in LBOs are American banks because their people, in Paris, have been trained in the techniques, or are familiar with the techniques that are used in this country. My firm in New York has shareholders who are European—French, German, and Italian—but we are currently working on an LBO in France, and we will probably end up with a syndicate of lenders led by U.S. banks. Also, U.S. banks are more motivated to get into the sophisticated high-value part of the business because they obviously do not have the commercial relations that the French banks or local banks have. They are forced to go into new areas, and actually what they are doing is really exciting. Citicorp has started a venture capital subsidiary, which has a very high visibility and is doing very well. Chase Manhattan has an excellent mergers and acquisitions department in Paris serving both French and U.S. clients. I consider Chase Manhattan my most dangerous competitor. U.S. investment banks are also extremely eager to get business in Europe in general and in France in particular. They bring a body of knowledge and expertise in the financial market that, I'm sorry to say, very few French institutions have. Dillon Reed is very active, Morgan Stanley has let several issues for French clients, and we are talking about $250 million for Peugeot and for L'Oréal. On top of that, the U.S. investment banks have an aggressive way of going after the client. The French financial community used to wait for the clients to knock at the door and say, "Look, next year I'm going to need a hundred million dollars." Morgan Stanley people don't do that; they study the company and then they come to you and say, "Look, next year you are going to need a hundred million dollars, and here is how we're going to get you the money now at the cheapest rate." So a significant portion of the revival of the French market is stimulated by foreign and especially U.S. institutions.

Two months ago I met an officer in a U.S. company, and because I was going to be in Paris the following week, he said, "Why don't you call my son; he works at Citicorp in Paris. He's a trader in short-term instruments." And I called the young man, once, twice, three times, just left my name and the name of my firm. And the fourth time, I left a message and explained to the secretary that I just want to have a drink with him because his father suggested it, and he picks up the phone and says, "Oh, I'm relieved, you know, because I get so many phone calls from French banks who are looking for traders in short-term instruments. Not to mention the headhunters." So if you have any expertise in short-term instruments trading you'll probably get yourself a job in Paris. However, I must tell you that they don't pay as well as in New York.

My approach is more of a lawyer's approach, and when I was asked the question about new French investment patterns, it took me a lot of time to find an answer. While I would agree with the fact that France is changing from a business viewpoint, I think it is more a psychological approach than a reality, because although there are substantial improvements, they are more of a psychological than a legal nature. And if you take some examples, such as the LMBO, you find out when you read the law carefully that the LMBO is a consensus reached between the business community and the French administration. You can imagine the result, which is, "You can do what you want provided you get my approval." The LMBO is a very attractive tool, but it is difficult in France to achieve the flexible LMBO that you have in the United States. In France, the process is long with the result that there have been few successful LMBOs in the last twenty months.

Similarly, exchange control regulations in France have been somewhat relaxed recently. With respect to doing business in France, exchange control regulations require that prospective investors in France must obtain approval of their investment plans from the Minister of Economy, failing which their plan falls through. The rules have been substantially modified and are now much more flexible, but still the principle remains that you are not free to invest the way you want to in French business.

A third example is labor law. In the United States you can hire anybody at any time, while in France employers are still subject to strong regulations that make it very difficult to terminate an employee, unless one provides substantial severance pay. So I think it's a kind of paradox: France is an attractive country for investors because of the new spirit of entrepreneurship, but on the other hand there are strict regulations which have changed only slightly.

Let me give you a last example. An American investor still has almost no possibility of making a successful tender offer because the ministry's approval is required before taking control of the company that is listed. In addition, one of the most important elements of a tender offer is secrecy, in other words the necessity of keeping the offer a secret as long as legally possible. However, in France you have so many parties intervening in the process that when you decide to proceed with a tender offer everybody is aware of it. And Paris is a small place. For these reasons, it is almost impossible for an American investor to make a successful tender offer in France without the cooperation of a French company or a French bank and the approval of the French administration.

How then can one invest in France without being hindered by the constraints I have just mentioned? The solution is to try a new approach. The American or foreign investor in France should take into account that France is now part of a market that is not limited to France, the European Economic Community. The advice I would give this investor is no longer to invest in France, but to do something in Europe with a presence in France. Today it is necessary to think in terms of a European rather than a French market, especially since European law is changing substantially. By 1992, Europe is really going to be a free market, which means that if you are in France you can invest in the Netherlands, you can do what you want in Germany and the United Kingdom; the European *marché unique* will be the biggest market in the world. So the solution in terms of finding new patterns for U.S. investors in France leads to the necessity of having a European approach to investment. I will give you an example to show you how it works. If you want to invest in France, you can do so through a European country with total flexibility. Let us assume that you want to acquire a company either alone or with other investors or with a French partner, and that the French shareholder of the company you want to acquire will keep up to 50 percent of the company. The new approach is to go to a holding company that is not a French company, but, for example, a Dutch company. This is step one. In step two, the Dutch company acquires an interest in a French business. The advantage of this system is, as mentioned above, flexibility: You have a holding company that is not subject to French corporate statutes.

French laws on corporations have not changed and do not permit the flexibility that you are used to in the United States, such as the shareholders' agreement. When you start a joint venture in the United States, you think immediately of a shareholders' agreement where you decide who is going to do what, who is going to own what, despite your interest and your percentage in the company. You may be willing to invest 80 percent of the purchase price and be a passive investor with no voting rights, or you may be the management of the company and have no money to invest but want 51 percent of the votes; that's almost impossible in France if you are dealing with a French holding company. However, if you go to a Dutch holding company, as in my example, or to a holding company in England or other Common Market countries then you automatically get this right back, which means that you can structure your corporate control the way you want. You can execute step one with another U.S. investor, and step two with a French investor, thus avoiding exchange control regulations. This is possible because a French investor who invests in the Netherlands with the intention of reinvesting in France is not subject to any exchange control approval, and as long as the American investor has 51 percent of the voting rights of the Dutch holding company, he or she is not subject to exchange control approval. This means that you have already taken care of the exchange control authorities, that you have taken care of the corporate structure of the company in terms of the decision-making process and financing, and that the holding company has the flexibility and corporate structure allowing it to invest in other countries in Europe besides France. Another advantage is that the requirement that employees participate in the management of the French company does not

apply to the foreign holding company that controls the French company. Therefore, you are not governed by the French legal system and retain the right to
decide on business strategy and investments in Europe without having to consult
the unions. French unions, as you may know, not only represent the employees
but are also strongly politicized and often oppose a business decision for non-
business reasons.

Thus the first advantage of the European holding company strategy is that it
allows you to be present in France without having to comply with French regulations. The second advantage is that this holding company offers you the
possibility of investing in other countries; by having your financial tools or your
corporate tools somewhere in Europe you can create another subsidiary or undertake another joint venture in Germany, in England, or in Italy, if you wish.
You also have the same flexibility as in the United States to take all the alternatives, including the alternative of going public and obtaining additional financing. Rather than making a tender offer on the French stock market, which
is very difficult for a foreign investor, you can go to the Dutch or the Luxembourg
stock exchange, and then you can go public with your French company indirectly.
With this system you raise money without, again, being subject to French statutes
for nonoperating areas.

Another example is the financial market. Although the French financial market
is attractive, it is not always as attractive as the Dutch market or the Eurodollar
market that you find in London, and in Luxembourg as well. The holding
company strategy thus presents the possibility of attracting money to your investment without being obliged to operate from France; this, again, gives you
the flexibility of having more players. Other investors feel safer because they
are not linked specifically to France. They like to be able to do something else
with their money and you have the tax advantages and the corporate structure
in terms of contracts this time.

Let's mention taxes and contracts. Usually subsidiaries of an American company in France have license agreements, technical service agreements, in consideration of which the parent company is paid the royalty on the business or
the sales of the French entity. There may be intellectual property rights, industrial
property rights, patents, know-how, trademarks over which you would want
absolute control. In addition, you would most probably want to maximize your
profit, which is perfectly normal. If it is the holding company that owns the
trademarks, the patents, and the know-how, then it is the holding company that
receives the royalty from the French company. A similar system can be structured
for all your subsidiaries in the world or in Europe. This uniform structure pleases
the tax people who love it when the taxpayer follows the same patterns over the
years in terms of corporate structure, where the money goes, and on which basis.
Setting a pattern that is acceptable from the tax viewpoint permits you to channel
money outside of the country, which is a concern of the foreign investors,
wrongly in my mind. This way of exporting money is legal and, again, not
subject to any exchange control approval. Finally, in the Netherlands, you get

the best of all worlds because it is a European country where you can get a tax rating and you are not subject to any income tax. So you have a flexible system that matches the market, which, in my opinion, is no longer only France but all of Europe. There is no harm in restricting yourself exclusively to France if you want to, but using the foreign holding company strategy gives you the possibility of continuing to expand to the European markets without losing the flexibility you need if you want to invest in a country or in the various countries that are substantially different from your own market, i.e., the U.S. market.

In summary, what I have said is not directly related to France, but presents my view of the new approach to investments in France, that is, keeping the business in France and exporting the corporate technology, the corporate know-how, and your corporate structure outside of France, but within Europe. The substantial change is that once you are in Europe you can do anything you want; you have no restrictions anymore. So there you have, in my opinion, what is currently, for some U.S. companies, the new pattern of investing in France while maximizing advantages of investment in all European countries.

DIALOGUE

QUESTION: Could the panelists talk a little bit about French investments in the United States?

ANGÉ: If you mean French companies doing business in the United States, strangely enough, this is the first time that there has been an increase of French investment in the United States at a time when the currency rate is favorable to the French. Previously, the French used to invest in the United States when it was very expensive and disinvest when it was very cheap, which meant a substantial loss for the French company. This year, strangely enough—maybe the French made a mistake—they are investing substantially in the United States, probably for currency reasons. A second interesting trend is that there is also an increase of joint ventures between French and American companies, because French companies have found that even with the best product in the world they lack the marketing expertise necessary for the U.S. market. And the second need they often have is for financing. For these reasons, French companies appear more and more willing to form a joint venture with an American partner who has two advantages: deep pockets and marketing expertise. It is too soon to say whether or not these joint ventures will succeed, because a minimum of five years is needed to decide if the marriage was good or bad. Joint ventures between U.S. companies often end up in disaster, so this may happen to U.S.-French joint ventures, also. However, the fact that the companies are on different continents may help the joint venture, because the companies are not competing on the same field. We have something that you don't have and you have something that we don't have. If you have two U.S. companies, each always believes that it has the same skills as the other.

QUESTION: In what areas do most joint ventures occur?

ANGÉ: In terms of numbers, I would say that most are in the high-tech industry, not only telecommunications but also in computers and software. Also, in some luxury product industries you have some French investments in the United States, some joint ventures in luxury products involving substantial amounts of money. I think joint ventures are not the traditional approach in the clothing business, nor in the financial market, but here you know better than I do.

QUESTION: Are French financiers, banks, and insurance companies investing to any great degree in the U.S. stock market?

ANGÉ: Absolutely. I can't give you the figures, but the answer is yes. Actually, it flows both ways. Part of the tremendous rise in stock prices that occured in Paris in '84, '85, and '86 also came from international investors, mainly U.S. funds. In Boston there are several funds that did extremely well overseas by investing in the Paris, Milan, and Amsterdam stock exchanges. On the other hand, there are many, many French investors in the U.S. market. In my firm, we have a clientele exclusively of European institutions for which we are brokers in the U.S. market. I can't obviously give you the figures but it amounts to large sums of money. And I would say that it is a permanent factor although it goes up and down; at one point, one of our clients had 200 million dollars, now they have something like one, but I am sure they will always remain on the New York stock market.

CARRERAS: I would just like to add one thing. There is now a new American instrument used for the French stock exchange and any other foreign exchange called the American Depository Receipt (ADR), which is a way to sell shares of a French company, listed on the French stock exchange, in the United States without dealing directly with the French stock exchange. The transaction emanates from New York with a custodial agreement; thus you have a representative, a financial institution in New York that shares the ADR, which gives you a title to a share of the French company, and that is becoming very successful.

QUESTION: Could Mr. Angé comment a little more on venture capital in France and financing for merging companies there, specifically on whether there has been some change recently in that area?

ANGÉ: Well, I'm not really an expert in that field. All I can say is that for many years venture capital has been an elusive dream for French financiers, more the object of talk than a realization. Actually, several financial institutions have set up special entities to try to provide seed money to emerging companies, but with very little success. What has been successful in France during the last fifteen years is development capital provided by institutions such as IDI or the British 3I (Investors in Industry) to companies that have already had a little success. At the seed money level, however, the problem has been recognized, and some tax incentives have been provided to enable investors to get more interested in this market. The creation of FCPR, which is a kind of mutual fund set up with a tax incentive on the condition that most of the money of the fund be invested in venture capital, has attracted the attention of a New York operator called Alan Patricoff Associates who now is manager of one of the first such

FDPRs. Citicorp, as I mentioned before, is also somewhat active in this area. However, I cannot give you a real expert opinion on the status of the venture capital industry in France. The FCPRs are only two years old, but I don't think they have been a tremendous success. There is still a problem in this area.

QUESTION: I'd like to address myself to Mr. Carreras' comments, and what I'd like to say is if I were a French business person I would not be very happy with your recommendations, with your comments about likely investment patterns. It reminds me of oil companies incorporated in the U.S in the early part of the century, first in New Jersey and Delaware to get around corporate taxes in other states, etc. So I'd like to ask you, what do you think the reactions of the French would be to these Dutch holding companies? Also, would a French company with a major foreign investor lose government subsidies?

CARRERAS: In answer to the first part of your question, I think that, on the contrary, the French companies or the French investors are more and more attracted by this system, by this structure. For two reasons: first, they feel it's an easy way to get partners who feel comfortable with investment and secondly, it's a way for them to understand that they can go beyond France and invest in Europe, a need that they understand more and more. Actually, the holding company is a tool which answers their concerns because they understand very often that five years from now they may disappear as a result of German competition on the French market. And the holding company approach is a way for them to get ready to do the same to the Germans and to protect themselves. So, from what I've seen, they like the idea, and some French companies even start this structure for themselves actually, without foreign investors.

In answer to the second question, which is, do you lose subsidies? Not at all. I was amazed to see the reaction of the exchange control authorities when we came up with this idea. The exchange control authorities said, "We understand perfectly what you mean, we fully agree, on the contrary, it's a very good idea, we approve." So I think there is a change of mentality, and, as I mentioned in the beginning, that is the paradox: There is a change of mentality but not yet a change of the statute. This allows us to anticipate what is going to happen in France in terms of corporate law changes that have not yet occurred.

ANGÉ: I should add that it is very good business for the lawyers to set up these holding companies in the Netherlands. Secondly, if I can risk a metaphor, someone yesterday mentioned to me that outside of Boston there is a small town that passed an ordinance barring the sale of liquor, so all around the city there are liquor stores. This is what it is like in France where the Treasury Department wants to keep its virtue but at the same time, business is business, so let the Dutch do the dirty work and at the same time, it's good business for Coudert Brothers, so why not?

QUESTION: What is the role of Paris as an international stock exchange and what is the power of French brokers?

ANGÉ: The major economic power is Germany, the second one in terms of GNP is France, Germany's main partner and client. For historical traditional reasons London is, obviously, the primary financial place in Europe; long before New York, it was, and might become again, according to what I hear on Wall Street, the number-one financial place in the world. But I don't think Paris is. In my view, no one in Paris would dare dream of supplanting London. London really remains the leading spot in Europe for financial activities. What the French people want is not to be eliminated. Let me give you an example. When Paribas was privatized the government imposed the period during which the shares of Paribas were not allowed to be traded in Paris on the Paris stock exchange. But the London brokers started trading in the Paribas shares that they did not own. They started a virtual market, which is what financial activities are all about: You're trading in concepts. So the government suddenly saw that the market was very bullish on the Paribas shares and before they were even sold, they were in London, trading up, up, up, up. So it created a problem because the government looked stupid selling the shares so low if the brokers in London were pushing them up. That is, in other words, what the French authorities and the French financial community do not want to see. They don't want to see all the French business, the issues in Eurofrancs, everything being handled in London. They want to have a little share of the business still in Paris.

QUESTION: Are American brokerage firms present in France?

ANGÉ: Most of the major brokerage houses from the United States are in Paris. If you read the Dennis Levine story maybe you recall that his first stint for Smith Barney was as the head of the Paris office. However, that's not where he learned his tricks, I can assure you. And Merrill Lynch, Shearson, all engage in brokerage activity in Paris. What I see in the European market in general is more U.S. banks becoming more and more active in Western Europe. Because of the Glass-Steagall Act they are barred from going into the securities industry here, but in Paris, in London, they can do whatever they want: trade in shares, do IPOs, LMBOs, everything. They have the power, they have the people, they have the will, and I would certainly say that Citicorp, Chase, Morgan Guaranty, and so on are going to be major players in the western European markets.

3

Privatization of Industry and the Media

Jean Loyrette
Pierre Barret

LOYRETTE

The French government born of the March 1986 elections has embarked upon a program of privatizations that, along with the British plan, is the most important that has ever been put in place in industrialized nations. The political result has essentially been two laws, one enacted in July 1986 and the other to be enacted shortly. The first provides for the privatization over five years of France's sixty-five largest companies, some nationalized in 1982, others in 1945–46 (when large insurance companies and banks had been nationalized).

This program's importance is underscored when we recall the role of the public sector in the French economy, a considerable role and one that is often not well understood outside the country. With the nationalizations of 1982, nearly the entire banking system, except foreign banks, was under state control. After 1945–46, about half the insurance sector was also state-controlled; in 1981–82, the great industrial sector—industries—was added to this state control. Five were nationalized directly, and the remainder were indirectly controlled. According to studies made by "L'Observatoire des Entreprises Publics," this meant that 25–30 percent of the industrial sector was involved—including service industries like transportation—or around 3,880–4,000 companies. Thus, the public sector was and is extremely important. Under the new financial plan, over the next five years, the state will have sold interests that are being valued between FF 250–300 billion. A considerable sum.

I shall begin by describing how this plan is put into operation—who is in charge of it. Then I shall examine the delicate problem of valuations of companies, of their shares and their payment. Finally, I shall address the economic forces that affect the market—the public, the companies, and foreigners.

Who is in charge of this plan of privatization? I believe that two ideas dominated the French legislature: to give to a few the authority to intervene; and to create a broad exposure for this program, since many in the opposition reproach the government for "selling off the national patrimony," or as former Prime Minister Macmillan said of Margaret Thatcher, "selling the family jewels." Thus, it is the government, specifically, the minister of finance, who decides the progression of privatizations of the sixty-five companies designated by law; under our constitution, a company cannot go from the public to the private sector without express legislative approval. The finance minister, then, chooses, and he has already selected two companies—Saint-Gobain and Paribas—and during the coming year is predicted to select a dozen more, representing between FF 40–50 billion. Once the finance minister has chosen a company, he can follow one of two procedures: a public offering that is addressed to the financial community via the Bourse, or a direct transfer process. This latter procedure, authorized by law, operates in particular situations; for example, companies who financially cannot or can barely make a public offering, like small or medium-sized banks, and for a certain number of specific operations. For example, the privatization of la Compagnie Générale de Construction Téléphonique (CGCT), which, recognizing its crumbling financial condition, was not interested in private investors, only in groups.

Once the finance minister has decided upon the privatization of a company, he can decide to create what is called an *action specifique*, which is the French version of what the British called a "Golden Share." This permits a symbolic representation for the state, since it limits participation to a certain level. This was the case for Elf-Aquitaine, where the minister decided that, without authorization, the maximum owner's cap would be limited to 10 percent. Further, in other very specific situations, especially those concerning national defense, an invester cannot have more than 5 percent interest in a company. This procedure has not yet been exercised. The "Golden Share" procedure was used only for Elf-Aquitaine and not implemented for either Paribas or Saint-Gobain.

Once these administrative decisions have been made, the process of privatization itself begins, which is complex and involves several steps. The first, for the idea of "exposure" earlier mentioned, is the valuation of the company. The government, in conjunction with various experts, develops a plan for an audit and selects those advisors who will be in charge of the valuation process. These advisors are well-known banks, including, on occasion, foreign banks. The valuation follows a precise procedure based on criteria established by the law authorizing privatizations and covers a company's market value, net assets, profitability, and future prospects. This is a financial analysis, and hence, banks with much experience in this area are called upon. For Saint-Gobain the banks were BNP (Banque Nationale de Paris) and Lazard; for Paribas, la Société de Banques Suisses. Also participating in this process are the company's bankers; that is, there is essentially a dialogue among those banks designated by the government and those by the company. When they arrive at a conclusion about the company's value, the information is presented to the Commission de Privatisations. This commission was established to ensure the credibility of all operations; I would say this is another example of the idea of "exposure." There are seven commissioners, named for five years, who have no direct involvement in the businesses; they function at the same time as top level civil servants and as presidents of large companies. They have a threefold mission. First, following the studies that are presented to them, they establish a minimum price; the minister is bound by this minimum price, but not to a higher one. And experience until now has shown that the finance minister has in both the Paribas and Saint-Gobain cases chosen a valuation slightly higher than that fixed by the commission.

The second mission is to advise the minister on the processes for transferring the state's investment to private investors—public, foreign, or individual. This is a more technical responsibility, and the minister is not automatically bound by the commission's suggestions, but he evidently tends to follow its advice. The final mission involves giving more general advice to the minister about privatization and the problems it entails.

Once the commission has fixed a minimum price, the minister publishes a notice in the *Journal Officiel*, that indicates the official commencement of the process. The process of privatization comprises several aspects, and I shall describe the case of Paribas, which until now has been the most interesting and complex example.

Paribas had capital composed of 75 percent shares that had been split because the face value was too high and 25 percent *certificats d'investissement*, which correspond to nonvoting shares. In the privatization law, the state is given great latitude in selling its stake in the company and can utilize all the classic commercial procedures; for example, the most currently used is a public market offering or a direct transfer outside the market to certain acquirers selected by the government. This implies an augmentation of capital in which, if the state owns 100 percent of a company, it renounces its right of application for shares and pulls back progressively; its participation diminishes as other participation increases. Such a method has not been applied, but it might in the future especially for insurance companies and for mergers or acquisitions, enabling the state progressively to become a minority interest and eventually sell all of its holding. To return to Paribas, the following procedure was used to deal with its 25 percent nonvoting shares and 75 percent voting shares and consisted of fulfilling three specific requirements. The law requires that 10 percent of the shares be automatically reserved for employees, and in the case of Paribas, employees applied for all the 10 percent available. Then the minister has the right—but not the obligation—to make an international issuing, which for both Paribas and Saint-Gobain represented 16–18 percent of each company's capital. This international offering followed normal procedures whereby French and foreign banks made available, in their respective geographical areas, shares to the international community. The remaining 45 percent, more or less, was offered to the public for sale, once again following standard procedures: shares are offered at a fixed price (there is no higher bid by definition) and, as was the case with Paribas, if there is an oversubscription, the number of shares is proportionally reduced. The final element that was introduced in the Paribas situation was what the constitution calls a "hard core" (*noyau dur*). This is a difficulty which, in my opinion, the government will have to confront on a case-by-case basis. I shall briefly explain.

It is not healthy for a company to have its capital totally dispersed. Three million shareholders, as the plan indicates, is attractive, but it is good for a board of directors or management to have a stable core of shareholders, a core of institutional, industrial, or financial investors who constitute a certain stability for the company. The trouble is that if you use the traditional method of a public offering, clearly it is impossible to gather together this stable core. If you want a stable group of 20 percent shareholders, and you have three million who are interested in becoming investors, you won't get it. Thus you are obliged to go outside the market and thus you become involved in a process that is necessarily one of discretionary choice by the government; it selects a certain number of investors that it assumes capable of stability and that will presumably bring something to the company. This occurred with Paribas. The minister reserved 20 percent of the shares for a group of seventeen investors, each of which received a fraction: this ranged from 3 percent for Compagnie Française des Pétroles Total, to 0.6 percent for certain other investors. For these investors, the minister imposed a fairly severe surcharge, which consisted of three elements. First, they had to pay more than what was offered per share in the public sale. In the case of Paribas this was a modest 2.5 percent, but for other cases, it was more; for example, in the latest bank to be privatized, a medium-sized bank, where the candidates are more numerous, the minister imposed a 45 percent surcharge for obtaining 51 percent of the capital. Hence, the rate is related to the number of those interested, the increase of participation, and the importance of the business.

The second element: The "core" that the investor has gathered must be conserved during at least two years. A profit cannot be realized immediately. A profit would be natural, as was shown with Paribas, when the price of shares rose rapidly; it would be irregular that the "hard core" investor who paid the 2.5 percent surcharge and gained 20 percent value in the following fifteen days would be allowed to sell. Where will the market be in two years? No one knows. The third element: If after the two years have passed the investor wants to sell his shares, it must offer them to the company on the market, and the company specifies a buyer. That is, it's a closed circle: The company has its say if the investor wishes to sell its participation.

What economic factors will have an impact on the market? First, evidently, there is the general public. The government uses a phrase that I do not much like: "popular capitalism." This journalistic or political expression masks an economic truth, which is that the powers that be want a great diffusion of shareholding among the French public. France is very late in this regard, and was even more behind a few years ago—I recall a statistic that indicated that only 1.5 million French directly owned shares, which is extremely low compared with other industrialized countries. The exceptional success of the privatization of Saint-Gobain and then Paribas is a good step forward, and one hopes that other privatizations will lead to a greater development of public shareholders. To encourage this trend beyond fiscal advantage, the government has provided that each French person as well as each foreign resident in France would have an automatic right to ten shares of a privatized company. For Paribas, where the number of people demanding stock was so great that there were not sufficient shares to take care of these ten shares, there was a proportional reduction, so that each person was given four rather than ten shares. For further incentives for this shareholding public, the government has provided another sweetener: The shareholder who keeps his stock for a year gets a free share.

The second economic agent is salaried workers, and this also reveals the intents of the government and legislature: to get employees interested in buying shares in their companies. Several years ago, a series of measures was put in place to encourage profit sharing. The results have been modest. The government's intention was to perfect, extend, and make this system more attractive. So it enlarged the definition of "salaried worker" to include not only current employees of a company, but those of a company's parent group; employees who had left the company less than five years earlier were included, as were some other groups. All these people are offered several advantages. First, they can purchase shares at a discount up to 20 percent. In the case of Paribas, the discount was 5 percent. In exchange for the discount, purchasers must retain their shares for at least two years. This is reasonable, since if someone is accorded a discount on day one, that person could turn around and sell his stock on the same day to get his 20 percent. Another advantage for these people is that they can arrange easy terms of payment for their purchase during a maximum of three years. These advantages encouraged salaried workers in both Saint-Gobain and Paribas to apply in great numbers for the 10 percent of the stock permitted them as a group.

Another area that poses many problems and which is the most complex in the privatization plan involves foreigners. The government wants, as it clearly stated before the legislature, that its interests not be sold in only a circular—or perhaps hexagonal—fashion; that the companies progressively become accustomed to foreign markets and be known in the international financial world. One of the great weaknesses of French industry and banking is that the number of companies that market their securities outside of France is very limited—nonexistent or symbolic, one might say. There have been many listings in the past and there are some today, but everyone knows these are symbolic. In the United States I believe there has only been one that has tried to be quoted, without brilliant results; there are some French companies but it is their American subsidiaries that are listed. In Japan there have been a few French companies listed and in Switzerland as well, but these could not be considered significant. Thus, the government wants to encourage companies to enter the international arena, and the best way of doing this was in a way that these securities become widespread in the international community, whether placed in banks or insurance companies. This was why care was taken with Saint-Gobain and Paribas to designate banks geographically—major banks from Switzerland, Germany, and Britain—and why the shares were spread out; and why the government created in these financial areas a secondary market with an exchange listing. But it confronted a problem, which was to provide an industry or a bank a certain protection that it will not be liable to direct or indirect control by foreign companies, which would threaten the privatization plan. For this reason, it was decided that the state could cede a maximum 20 percent of its interest to foreigners; in the cases of Saint-Gobain and Paribas, this had been 16 percent and 19 percent respectively because the flood of French orders obliged the foreign participation to be slightly reduced. This is the problem when the state sells its shares, and it often leads to confusion: Not only can foreigners not acquire more than 20 percent of a company, but further, a distinction must be made between a company or a group working together to acquire 20 percent. In the latter case, authorization is needed.

Investors who have no ties between them can go beyond 20 percent, and there certainly are many companies on the Paris Bourse with more than 20 percent foreign investors. The more delicate problem involves the relationship between the privatization plan and the Brussels Commission, i.e., the European Economic Community. The EEC shares, in principle, the concept of free trade, and that implies free investment; thus there is the potential of having EEC investors acquire, without limit, shares in a French company in cash, or having a controlling interest in it or all of its capital. The commission has already faced this issue. When the British government created its famous Golden Share, the commission reacted critically, for it was a way, albeit an elegant one, of limiting foreign investors in their tentative attempt to take control, since by definition they were unable to go beyond a certain percentage. In the French situation, the government by law can impose on certain companies a maximum limit of participation of 10 percent in cash. But there is no discrimination: This applies to French investors as well as those from the EEC. In Elf-Aquitaine, the minister forbade everyone to have without authorization more than 10 percent—French and foreigners alike.

The EEC issue is on two levels. On one level, for years there has been a difficulty interpreting terms between the commission and the French Treasury. The commission tends to say: "A company controlled by European investors means a company in which 50 percent or more of the investors are from the EEC." This makes sense, for otherwise you could have a Japanese or American company create a Dutch company, have a 100 percent interest in it, and say: "But we are an investor in the Common Market." The trouble is that the French

Treasury has shown itself to be more restrictive and considers that 50 percent is not sufficient; that a company in the Common Market cannot be considered in the Common Market if it cannot prove that 80 percent of its capital is controlled by investors of the Common Market. For the major multinational companies that are listed on many exchanges this poses absolutely insoluable problems. Unilever or Royal Dutch, for example, could not say whether 80 percent of their shareholders are residents of the Common Market. Thus, limiting foreign participation to 20 percent poses considerable problems for the commission. This particular issue has not yet arisen, but the commission has notified the government that if the situation does arise, because of its obligations regarding the Treaty of Rome, France could not oppose actions over 20 percent, and especially regarding a controlling interest. The only exception is in areas precisely spelled out in Article 233 of the treaty, in the domain of national defense and public security—which, for example, protects businesses like Dassault or Thomson, that evidently work for France's national defense.

Another program, which has yet to begin but should be underway in five years, is the privatization of communication. Another program concerns the privatization of Crédit Agricole, one of the largest banks in the world, and which is regulated by special law. Its privatization will essentially be a special case. So there is a movement of privatizations in place, and for the moment this has been a successful program, which is a surprise even for those who are following the situation closely. If one had made a survey before the privatization of Paribas, asking the experts "How many stockholders of Paribas will there be," I would have answered 500,000. Certainly never 3.5 million, and I believe this is the case for other experts as well. This incontestably indicates a great change in the mentality of the French public, in the widest possible sense. And not just for the property-owning public, which is generally older, but for the young middle manager, and even, to the great amusement of Paribas, for students; the latter purchased Paribas stock. This has been an evolution, not a revolution in thinking. Will it be deep, or is it a flash in the pan? We have had unfortunate experiences in the past, for example, what were called the REP (sociétes de récherche petrolière—oil exploration companies). People would line up at 4 A.M. in front of banks to buy some REP shares; then things went wrong, especially in the Sahara. The stock's value was slightly better than the Russian loan, but not by much. Will the infatuation last? There has been what one might call a leap-frogging. Those who bought four shares of Saint-Gobain sold them to buy four shares of Paribas, which were sold for four shares of X. No one knows, but I believe that the mass of buyers is such that certainly a significant portion of them will remain attracted to the market, a portion that is clearly larger than that seen in the past.

One final important point: We must take into account the absorption capacity of the financial market. The government must be alert to the market and follow public reaction, not fix its plans solidly for the next several years. Things must be done progressively. If already by 1987, seven or eight operations have been realized, this spells success. Several important companies would remain, but these would follow if the political situation is stable in the coming years.

Privatization will have an important impact on the evolution of businesses in France. It is not a panacea; it will not give firms all the vigor and dynamism needed, but it will push them in that direction. State protection will be partly suppressed; employees will become more involved, which is a fundamental point; those companies that have been privatized will become more flexible and dynamic—for one of the perverse effects of insularity is what has been called "the glaciation of the public sector." In other words, as soon as a company entered the public sector it congealed, and unless it committed an infraction, the public sector had great difficulty selling it and buying another. This rigidity was excessively damaging for large companies. And I think that the possibility of returning to the public sector will oblige them to submit to the strong winds of competition.

DIALOGUE

MODERATOR: Mr. Loyrette, your presentation of nationalization was very interesting but very technical. From your talk, one would assume that this is a straightforward financial operation. But it occurs to me that the debate since 1981 over nationalization and privatization is a purely political one. The processes of nationalization of companies and their subsequent privatization have nothing to do with a strategic or business reasoning; they are purely political maneuvers. Even the process which you describe so brilliantly is merely a political process. The state determines which companies will be privatized when; who will be allowed to buy what percentage of shares; and which companies or groups will constitute the hard core or *noyau dur*. The liberal discourse of the Chirac government masks a *dirigiste* privatization where many of the traditional Gaullist groups are being rewarded with controlling blocks of stock. But where does this leave the newly privatized companies? Will they be more competitive as a result of this process? Won't this just further jeopardize their financial position since proceeds of the sale of the shares will go to the state and not to the companies?

LOYRETTE: Yes, all important economic debates are also political. But you are both right and wrong. You are absolutely correct when you underscore that the state plays an important role: It is the owner of the shares and therefore the seller. It is up to the state to decide what happens. Its role is therefore considerable. But it is important that the state play this role and defend the national interest.

We are living through a transition period and this is only the first step. The state has put its holdings up for sale and will retain its hard core of investors. But this is only for two years. At the end of these two years, what will happen? Perhaps with good management, the companies' performance will improve and the value of the shares will increase. In this case, the hard core investors may hold on to their investment or even increase their holdings. But if the companies' financial results were mediocre, the core investors could break up, and institutions and individuals could sell. With a major public offering, some investors could gain 20 percent, 30 percent, or even 40 percent control of the companies. Who knows? But for now, the government has wisely chosen to proceed slowly, to monitor the sales, and control of the distribution of the stock.

QUESTION: But haven't French companies been submitted to government controls like these since the war?

LOYRETTE: Yes, companies have been controlled in the past, but the old form of controls were price controls and exchange controls. Nationalization, too, was unhealthy for business. For example, in banking, the insufficient funds of French nationalized banks is often criticized. This was not because these banks were poorly managed, but because since 1956, the state has not performed its proper duty as the shareholder. Over thirty or forty years, there has never been an increase in capital. So what are they supposed to do? If they had been in the private sector and were well managed, these banks could have raised their capital; if they had not been well managed, they would have had to make other choices. But when there are government controls, the market mechanisms and sanctions cannot function.

QUESTION: You have noted that one of the problems of French firms is their insufficient capitalization. But the French privatization process does not return any of the funds generated by the sale to the companies themselves; instead the money goes to general state revenues.

LOYRETTE: This is one of the criticisms currently being made of the privatization process. The proceeds from the sale of the state's holdings will improve the state budget deficit but they will also be used to subsidize other public enterprises that are not doing well. But the newly private companies can also go to international financial markets to raise the needed capital. Once again, the state must protect the larger national interest.

BARRET

There is a story of a foreign tourist who was lost in a remote district of Paris and asked a policeman the way to the Arc de Triomphe. Said the policeman: "You start from here . . . at the end, you turn left, then the second right after the dead end . . . you cross the boulevard . . . No! That's too complicated! Instead, start this way, follow the boulevard until the second subway station . . . No! That's not direct, you won't be able . . . " He then looked at the tourist sententiously, saying, "You know, sir, to get to the Arc de Triomphe, you shouldn't start from here."

At least two lessons can be drawn from this tale. First, regulation of the audiovisual media in France has for too long a time been irrational, and a simple reform cannot quickly create a rational, updated, and satisfying organization for listeners and viewers. Second, it is extraordinarily difficult to explain to foreigners what is happening today in the French audiovisual area if they do not know its recent history. This history is part of a political world that in the past entirely controlled radio and TV, and that, during the last five or six years, has been trying to relinquish its hold with some sincerity but with evident apprehension and some ulterior motives.

During a generation—about thirty years—this total power was maintained in the interest of the state, even while the communications industry was developing. For example, in 1953 half of France was waiting to be connected to the telephone system while the other half waited for their telephones to work; 99 percent of the households had no television. But already the state was involved in TV's beginnings. Successively, it controlled from creation the first, second, and third TV channels. In addition, it controlled the company that broadcast them (Télédiffusion de France, TDF); the company that produced nearly everything the channels did not themselves produce (Société Française de production, SFP); the company serving as an archive for programs and which managed their rights, (Institut National de l'Audiovisuel, INA). The state also controlled all public companies whose directors were political appointments; television channel presidents were also appointed by the government, i.e., the cabinet ministers. This control was maintained until 1982, when the companies were reorganized.

We sometimes forget that the state's role, once absolute in television, has also been very strong in other communication areas. The state is also far and away the first customer of Agence France Presse (AFP), whose influence, as the first supplier of information for all French media, is substantial. One of the major stockholders of the second largest information agency, Agence Centrale de Presse (ACP), is a public company.

The state controls, partially or entirely, all radio. It totally controls public radio, Radio France with France Inter, France-Culture, France Musique, Radio France Internationale, Radio France Outre-Mer, and others of lesser importance. It partially controls all other radio, because aside from public radio, financed primarily by taxes, the state has permitted four commercial stations to develop through a private statute, a permission that in appearance is more liberal but that in fact is a monitored freedom. The law designates these stations as "peripheral," allowing them to broadcast on long wave toward France, with transmitters located outside national territory. The four are: RTL, from Luxembourg; Europe 1, from the Sarre (a result of a postwar agreement with West Germany); Radio Monte Carlo, from Monaco; and Sud-Radio, from Andorra. These stations have offices and studios in Paris from where programs are transmitted by cables, under public control, to their transmitters located beyond France's borders.

The state retains control of director appointments, sometimes even of some journalists, as is the case with television. Further, it does not hesitate to change them, depending on new political majorities or dominant political sentiments.

Finally, the state has a majority participation in Havas, the major French advertising company in posters; thus it has advertising influence in daily papers, magazines, peripheral radio, publicity in movie theaters, and even on buses and the subway.

Not until 1981 was this massive state control questioned, first by the Left, then by the new majority after the March 1986 elections. The consequences of these two waves of deregulation, with their political calculations, are still not very well understood; the entire French information and media market has been shaken. The first move in this chess game will be made with the assigning, for ten years, of TF1 (channel 1, which is the principal organ for news and advertising in the country), to one of two candidates. Already we can count the victims, the first naturally being those who did not get what they wanted. But there are other victims among those who got satisfaction, and probably there will be more in this so-called privileged group sharing the biggest parts of the pie that has just been distributed. The pie, in fact, may be much less sweet than they imagined.

A lot of money has been spent. During the past two years lobbying was the favorite sport of communication directors. We saw the biggest become allies, then betray each other in a matter of weeks, or days. Some are reaching the finish line with wounds, lighter illusions, and heavier handicaps for the future. France, a country of 55 million, without having clearly decided for itself, finds itself with five general national channels plus a pay channel for movies, all of which will depend on advertising. The same is true for the 1,000 local radio stations that did not exist six years ago. Meanwhile, there are two contentious appeals to annul the decree or the assigning of concessions. Furthermore, the current political opposition [the Socialists] threatens to erase everything and start from scratch if it is returned to power.

We can see how we got into this situation in some brief episodes.

Before becoming president, Mr. Mitterrand had been indicted for his involvement in an FM radio station broadcasting from Paris, which was an infringement of the law. Once in power, in 1981, he quickly announced the end of the monopoly shared by the public radio and the four peripheral stations; a few months later 1,200 new stations were created, many overlapping, to the great despair of a powerless and overwhelmed allocation committee. Advertising was prohibited, although stations emerged that disguised their use of it. Then, advertising was permitted, but with broadcasting frequency limitations. We now see those who do not respect those limits increasing (using up to fifty times authorized broadcasting power). Networks are forbidden, but practically the only stations that can survive economically are those in networks.

Since 1982, as a result of a new audiovisual organization law, the state's monopoly has been breaking down, though it retains a dominant position and maintains a strong public role. The law provided for instituting a commission (Haute Autorité de l'Audiovisuel), which was granted many powers including appointing the directors of the public enterprises in this sector.

Would this be the dawn of a new independence from political influence for these channels? Not yet. In the new commission, three members, were appointed by the president of the Republic, three by the president of the Senate, three by the Socialists, and three by the opposition Right. As they could be removed and had been appointed for nine years, some would need a long time to shed their original political colors. But it's fair to say that things evolved with the times, and the Haute Autorité proved to be more ecumenical in its choices and more independent in its public positions by 1985.

The next decision, made in 1983, was the creation of a new "coded" (i.e., pay) television channel, which would be private and have a powerful national broadcasting network. The channel could show a great number of movies, more than other channels, but its revenues would have to come through subscriptions and some public sponsorship.

Following traditional wisdom, the channel was entrusted, with no public offering, to the Havas agency, in which the state has a majority interest, surrounded by several major nationalized banks. The Socialists enacted a mixed public/ private law, which would also be imposed on future companies involved in cable networks. Canal Plus, the new pay channel, was born on 1 November 1984. A few months later, Mr. Mitterrand announced that a review of frequencies would begin. It was speculated that he might allow the creation of two national private networks that would operate alongside the three public channels. The idea of free programs financed by advertising brutally interrupted Canal Plus's subscription sales. By spring of 1985, the Paris "establishment" considered the new channel near bankruptcy. But its head, a close friend of Mr. Mitterrand, got permission to broadcast "uncoded" for several hours a day, and to have commercials during these periods, especially during prime time—6:00 to 8:30 P.M.

By the summer of 1985, one spoke less of the new private channels for their concessions would not be granted before the end of the year. Subscriptions for Canal Plus began to take off: There are nearly two million subscribers today, at

$300 each per year; advertising revenues are no longer negligible, and results are brilliant for its third year of activity.

In the fall of 1985 things were once again in turmoil, as the election neared. In November, without a true public offering, a quasi-public–quasi-private network, the fifth channel, under very privileged circumstances, was granted to Jérome Seydoux and Christophe Riboud, who have close ties to Mr. Mitterrand; their associates included Silvio Berlusconi, king of television in Italy. Soon thereafter, the second, more limited network, was granted to two other operators at the initiative of the then prime minister, Laurent Fabius. This sixth channel, TV 6, was to be thematic and musical in the style of MTV to avoid a heavy drain on the advertising market. The new operators began broadcasting in February 1986, a few weeks before the general elections.

In its campaign, the Right clearly stated its position: If it won the election, it would privatize two of the three public channels and reexamine the assigning of channels 5 and 6. No one spoke too much of Canal Plus, for its owner, Mr. Rousselet, skillfully reduced Havas's capital to 25 percent and brought in new French and foreign private shareholders.

A few days before the election, President Mitterrand made a final effort and privatized the second national peripheral radio station, Europe 1, which I had the honor of directing; the state's majority interest was sold to the Hachette group. Then on 16 March 1986, the Left lost the election, and the strange cohabitation between President Mitterrand and Prime Minister Chirac began.

The new majority quickly struck with a deep reform in the audiovisual area: a new law that promised to open things up. This law, which encountered many difficulties in being put together, was not finally passed until fall 1986. But what chaos! The first public TV channel, TF1, would be immediately privatized and the third channel would be shortly thereafter. The concession granted to channels 5 and 6 would be cancelled, and an indemnity price would be determined; the authorizations to run these networks would be granted to new operators following a public offering approach.

The organization in charge of executing this ambitious program would not be the Haute Autorité, whose members theoretically could not be removed (but who would be sent home), but a new group: the Commission Nationale de la Communication et des Libertés (CNCL). This group would have thirteen members— two named by the president of the Republic; two by the president of the Senate; two by the president of the Assembly; one by the Supreme Court of Appeal; one by the Council of State (Conseil d'Etat); one by the Audit office (Cour des Comptes); and one by the French Academy (Académie Française). These ten would appoint three other members on the basis of their expertise in telecommunications, the press, and television. This is a shrewd combination. Even if this group, like its predecessor, demonstrates an initial docility toward the power that established it, the hope is that it will, in time, find the path of cohesiveness and independence.

The concession of channels 5 and 6, canceled by decree, would cease broadcasting on 28 February 1987 at midnight. The new operators would begin on March 1. The former licensees are appealing in court. One can hardly imagine what will happen if, after a long trial, the court one day decides in their favor.

Behind the scenes, all the communication groups interested by the reassigning of concessions for channels 5 and 6 and the privatization of the first public channel (TF1) were frantically agitating to show themselves in the best light with the best alliances. The CNCL received two proposals for channel 5; three for channel 6; and two for TF1. Those betting on the commission's political docility predicted that the concessions would be granted this way: channel 5 to Mr. Hersant; channel 6 to Mr. Monod and the CLT; TF1 to Mr. Lagardère, president of the Hachette group.

In a few weeks, this diagnosis proved correct in the first two cases; the third decision will be made shortly. One is tempted to agree with those who claim everything is decided in advance in spite of the call for public hearings. But this may not be correct or is at least exaggerated, for several reasons:

—For channel 5, Mr. Hersant's record, technically, was the strongest.

—It took several votes to obtain a majority for the concession of TV 6, an indication of a vigorous internal debate in the commission. The problem was choosing between general and musical programming, as happened in 1986. This was legitimately discussed because of the limits of the advertising market.

—For TF1, it is expected that 10 percent of the stock will be reserved for employees, 40 percent for the public, and the operating group will have to pay FF 3 billion for the remaining 50 percent; no stockholder can retain over 25 percent. This price is considered very high for a risky license of ten years.

The political favorite for this last license is the Hachette group, but there are many voices raised even in the majority to warn against such a decision, which would result in an unprecedented concentration of power in advertising and news. Hachette and its associates indeed control several dailies, dozens of magazines, the second national network of radio, and several secondary networks in terms of frequency; they control the second largest poster company and have the entire distribution of the press. The group is by far the leading publisher and distributor of books, with numerous companies, and it is already a producer in audiovisual areas, using its own studios as well as fixed and mobile equipment.

Mr. Raymond Barre has well expressed what public opinion generally resents, declaring: "It is in the name of freedom of communication that the state should disengage from this sector. It is also in the name of the same principle that it must, as much as possible, enable new parties to profit from this disengagement. An excessive media concentration threatens pluralism of expression."

For its part, the Constitutional Council (Conseil Constitutionnel) made a similar point, stating:

The licensing by the CNCL must take into account . . . the triple necessities of diversity of operators, assuring pluralism of opinion, and avoiding the abuse of a dominant opinion.

And more precisely, the commission must ensure that concentration in the communication sector is limited when selecting a group of acquirers.

So, this is the state of affairs to date. The decisions made or expected will not solve everything. As communication is increasingly international, many of these national policies are becoming illusory. One can, in Paris, with a satellite dish, receive CNN, and very soon with only a slight delay watch Dan Rather on Canal Plus. The British are developing new satellite programming that can easily be viewed in France. Meanwhile, France continues its game of political control of the audiovisual sector, superimposing national quotas on production and broadcasting; for nearly ten years, the government has debated with itself whether it should launch its own powerful satellite. With such a game, no political party wins, but the industry loses a lot. France historically has often awakened after the war. I hope this is not the case for the audiovisual industry. I think that the tourist who asked a policeman for directions would be better to take a taxi. If he went on foot, he risks arriving at the Arc de Triomphe after the battle . . .

I have summarized some very agitated years. The surprises will not end after the presidential election of 1988, I suspect. The best situation would be that the political world would cede to the private audiovisual sector the wisdom of the CNCL and the initiative of entrepreneurs.

Moreover, the Fates have just winked. The CNCL recently moved to a beautiful building on 56 rue Jacob in Paris. A marble plaque near the door reads: IN THIS BUILDING, FORMERLY THE YORK HOTEL, ON 3 SEPTEMBER 1783, DAVID HARTLEY IN THE NAME OF THE KING OF ENGLAND, BENJAMIN FRANKLIN, JOHN ADAMS IN THE NAME OF THE UNITED STATES OF AMERICA, SIGNED THE FINAL PEACE TREATY RECOGNIZING THE INDEPENDENCE OF THE UNITED STATES.''

So, why not the beginning of the independence of the French audiovisual sector two hundred years later?

DIALOGUE

QUESTION: My question concerns the frequencies used by French radio broadcasting today: How are the radio bands divided, and could an American use his American receiver to receive French radio programs?

BARRET: In the past in France we used long, medium, small, and short waves; it was very complicated, not consistent with international standards, and there was no FM. Then, FM broadcasting grew, and even stations that were previously transmitting only long waves because of regulation, the peripheral stations I mentioned earlier, now broadcast in FM. As a consequence, even with equipment made in Japan, for example, it is possible to hear them, which was not the case before. The situation is not perfect, however, because the receivers' frequency bands do not always correspond to the frequencies allocated, particularly for FM; the receivers don't have bands that are wide enough. This is complicated and technical, and I don't want to give inaccurate information. I believe that many receivers are limited to 104 cycles while the assigned frequencies go up to 108. So, there are still some problems and wrinkles to be ironed out, but normally, you would be able to receive all stations.

QUESTION: What is the influence of English broadcasts on France—its language and culture?

BARRET: Often we are put off by cultural imperialism in its linguistic form, that is, as if language were the principal vehicle of culture. I believe this is too restrictive. In fact, a program translated, adapted, and presented in French is a stronger vehicle in French than in the original language, first because it is available to all the population rather than only a few people, and also because it delineates a mindset, mental projections, and social attitudes. So, I believe there are two major issues. First, how many French people will be able to receive English-speaking programs directly. For the short term this number is small because some English-speaking programs will be broadcasted only via cable, and in France, cable is very late in coming. Other programs will be via satellites, which implies receiving equipment for viewers, and this is not developed on a large scale in France today. On the other hand, French TV, like nearly all European television, uses a lot of American programs, which are adapted and dubbed. This means American series like "Falcon Crest," "Dallas," "Dynasty," "Little House on the Prairie," "Moonlighting," and so forth. There are probably twenty I could name, and these top twenty are shown on one of the six channels. This is a sensitive point for the CNCL, and a principal justification of its role and intervention and its spelling out the conditions for new operators of channels 5, 6, and TF1. These superimposed conditions are draconian and concern quotas of original French-created programs and their production. Such quotas have economic consequences for these channels. This is why I said earlier that some channels didn't fully consider the economic impact of this side of operations, which will be more difficult than they expected.

Take TF1, for example. Concerning "fiction," that is, exclusively programs running fifty-two minutes (roughly, an hourly series): To have 50 percent of your programs consist of French-produced series requires about 85 percent of your production budget, while the remaining 15 percent can cover purchases of American series for the other half of your programming. Hence, it is an obvious temptation to buy American programming, in part because it is inexpensive, and also because it is efficient: It has been widely and thoroughly tested, and its ratings are good, in France as elsewhere. The problem is one of market size. That is, a production originating in the United States can amortize its costs over a wide audience; one originating in France cannot.

The solutions to this are difficult. One possibility is European coproductions. This is more difficult than it looks on paper, first for cultural reasons. There are few subjects whose treatment can be agreed on by the Italians, English, German, and French. Second, there is some American protectionism to deal with. It is nothing direct, but it too is draconian: It is practically impossible to sell a program in the United States that was not originally in English, or rather, American; sometimes there are even hesitations about accents from Oxford and Cambridge. So, a French program is impossible: If you produce a good French series and dub it in English and try to sell it in the United States, you'll be turned down. So, in all cases, the first condition for a series, even a European one, is that it at least be recorded for original issue in English. It is natural for European countries to be concerned about their cultural protection in this regard; the economic repercussions are such that it would be a great temptation for entrepreneurs to choose the easy way: to opt for Anglo-Saxon programs.

QUESTION: What is happening with the satellite companies—Société Française de Production, INA, TDF? And what is your opinion about the advertising: Will all the channels be able to sell advertising at the same time—and what is the survival rate in an environment that may not be able to support all of them?

BARRET: Regarding your first question, I wish the politicians had asked that, for I suspect the issue didn't receive any serious attention. For TDF there will be relatively few changes as all the operators are going to use TDF's services; but one can foresee a better balance in their relationships. That is, there are pressures by the operators to improve TDF's productivity and attempts to get broadcasting contracts that are closer to the kind you get in a private organization. We'll never reach this point completely, primarily because—especially for the big channels, e.g., TF1—telebroadcasting has been such an engineering success. This is a typical French situation. In France we have a Hertzian frequency network of unbelievable density. [The French use the term "Hertzian" for the electromagnetic waves used in radio and television transmission.] There are more Hertzian transmitters on French territory (550,000 square kilometers) than in all of the United States. Why? Because this goes along with our idea of public service, which insisted that every French person anywhere could receive the three public TV channels—and we'd make sure he could by installing sufficient transmitters. You can imagine the cost of ensuring reception to every last farm or summer house in the Alps, Pyrenées, and Massif Central. The result was too many broadcasters and that cable was never born out of a spontaneous need, as was the case in the United States. In the United States, cable arose because some people could not receive television, and they gathered in groups to install various kinds of local systems. This didn't happen in France because everyone could, via Herztian frequency, receive television transmission. As a consequence, broadcasting costs are obviously very high. To give you an idea of the scale, the cost of TF1, which will have to be carried by the new operator as part of the deal, is over FF 550 million per year. This is enormous.

Another result is the overconsumption of the Hertzian frequencies. These frequencies are scarce resources. If you create an extremely dense network in a country, you consume a lot of frequencies because for each rebroadcast you must use a different frequency from the original relay. For example, if in Paris, the Montparnasse Tower creates a "shadow zone" for the Eiffel Tower, you must retransmit behind the Montparnasse Tower, but with a different frequency from the one used to carry TF1, A2, or FR3. So, to cover all our territory we used a great quantity of frequencies, and this explains why there are so few left in nearly all the major French cities. Some other countries have done the same thing, so we have a very serious problem in border areas where public systems face each other: the French-German border, the French-Belgian border, and part of the French-Italian border.

Concerning the advertising issue. I am not particularly qualified to have a better opinion than others, but after many years devoted to this topic, I think we are in a very dangerous situation for the television operators. I don't think the French market can support the weight of six channels calling for commercials to different degrees. Hence, I think one of them is doomed, one way or another, although it's not clear today which one. All the operators have the financial capability of holding on for a long time, which is disturbing because other media will suffer. I would be concerned if I operated a peripheral radio network or were a magazine publisher, especially a mass-market publication, for these are vulnerable. This is also true for dailies. I think the French advertising market probably cannot sustain six channels, and if it does, this will seriously disturb the other media.

QUESTION: I wonder if privatization is real, or is the government retaining an important influence, even if by indirect means.

BARRET: I suspect that all politicians, regardless of their political stripes, want to maintain privileged relationships with the audiovisual sector. I would emphasize that this has never worked; it was always the political power controlling TV that lost the next election. So, they should wake up and realize that they should let the press work in peace so it can do its job.

Now, to answer your question. I believe that some steps are important, even if they're not perfect, like establishing an independent commission. It may not be very independent at the outset, but with time, it will distance itself from the political power that created it. I also believe in having a public sector. Personally I hope that we can keep two public channels, for I think it would be very dangerous to have only one in France, as the ultraliberals were hoping after the 1986 elections. This would weaken the public sector. I also believe it would be more balanced and healthy to have only four TV channels: two public and two private. Hence, I hope that another public channel will not be privatized.

You are essentially correct that all political powers still hope to keep privileged relationships through private operators. And I believe this continues, although differently from past interventions. Television operators now have sufficient economic concerns that they do not want to create political problems for themselves. Hence, at least for the short term, even if they have some sympathy for those who appointed them, in the long run, the operators, whoever they may be, will have to be entrepreneurs first, especially in the general channel. They will have to manage well, and, as generalists, they will be more or less condemned to pluralism, to some kind of freedom of expression. The opposite attitude would be in contradiction to the economic interest of the channel.

Thus, the establishment of an independent commission and the fact of having private operators alongside a public sector seem to me like good steps, even if these steps were not taken entirely without ulterior motives.

QUESTION: What is your opinion on the impact of the Common Market, particularly 1992, on television and on the possibility of foreigners having interests in the French market?

BARRET: I think that private television networks will increasingly become businesses like any other and will, as a consequence, reflect a freedom of movement. I am much more cautious about the area of programming. European television is an old dream, an old fantasy, which regularly reappears. It once appeared in the form of the famous seventh channel. Mr. Pierre Desgraupes, a highly qualified man, was commissioned to study what could be a satellite channel with a European cultural orientation. I think Mr. Desgraupes conducted a very thoughtful study and clearly exposed the issues; I'm sure he didn't underestimate the difficulties. As I mentioned earlier, just to create an international program is extraordinarily difficult. It's much easier to organize a "stock exchange" of national programs. You take programs created in Italy and broadcast them in France, rather than trying, at any cost, to make international coproductions.

Concerning advertising, the brands that rigorously employ the same strategy, same packaging, same distribution, etc., are limited, perhaps around eighty to one hundred. Thus, those interested in advertising on a channel that had identical programming in France, Belgium, Italy, and Germany are too small in number. I think it is unrealistic to envision this kind of programming in the coming years.

Finally, I think the freedom of motion I mentioned will have many consequences. There will be exchanges of creators, authors, directors, and so forth, as well as on the level of capital; there will also be changes in ownership of the various communication media. I am not so sure that this will happen as quickly at the programming level.

QUESTION: I would be curious to know the attitude or feelings of average French people vis à vis all these new changes. What do they expect? What do they hope for? Will they be disappointed?

BARRET: They were not much consulted. Their opinion wasn't sought, so we only partially know. An interesting point, perhaps, is that a large majority is currently against TF1's privatization. This fact is absolutely astonishing, and I believe that it would not be the case if the first channel to be privatized were FR3, although the public might hold the same opinion about Antenne 2. The government hesitated a long time before choosing which channel to privatize, and I believe that one of the reasons that the majority of the French are against TF1's privatization is that this channel has experienced a spectacular recovery during the last two or three years. This means that the public is very satisfied with it now; that is, it now has the kind of programming that pleases the public, which is rather concerned about changes. When you run in-depth studies you can see that the public credits the private sector with some virtues, like more creativity, imagination, doing new things, and so forth. But it also attributes some dangers to it, most notably, slicing up programs with commercials.

Actually, TF1 has a sort of intermediate status, in that it approaches being a privately run channel. It does not cut up movies, series, or news programs with advertising. It is in a strange situation now, for it is successful commercially and has a lot of advertising to broadcast, which it blocks into "advertising screens," some of which are quite lengthy. Broadcasters in the United States would laugh at this, for in the states you have interruptions that are frequent but that last around two minutes or two minutes and thirty seconds. On TF1 the "advertising screens" can last seven minutes. Happily, French commercials are made well enough and are more tolerable than their American counterparts, but seven minutes of advertising is nonetheless unendurable. So, this situation is transitory and will change. I don't know how the French public will welcome the first commercial interruptions in their programs, but probably they won't like them much on TF1; they would be more welcome on the fifth or sixth channels, as part of the logic of being private. If it's a new channel, one can accept these interruptions because one is not obliged to watch the programs, but TF1 is an institution. It was the first public channel, with the biggest audience; it represents a bit of the national heritage in people's minds. Therefore, people will probably have more difficulty accepting this addition to something that is already in a form that pleases them.

QUESTION: Do you see the television tax being reduced?

BARRET: There has already been a reduction, and in my view that was a big mistake, an act of political cowardice. This tax in France is too low to provide for the grand ambitions of public service. Many successive governments have refused to increase the tax, which should have been raised; it is much lower than other such taxes in Europe. I consider that refusal as similar to the reduction in the tax just at the moment of privatizing. This was a symbolic gesture, but I believe it's a bad symbolism, for one thing is certain: If you want quality television, you have to recognize that it's not free and there are several ways of paying for it. You can have a tax, a subscription process, or commercial interruptions. But it is very bad to let people think that a program is free to them, because that's the best way to make poor quality programming.

QUESTION: There are many French people in the United States who receive Radio-France Internationale. If this kind of radio is privatized, am I correct in assuming it will be nearly impossible to receive it?

BARRET: Exactly. But this is absolutely not on the agenda. I don't think anyone in France would dream of actually suggesting it. When I spoke of ongoing privatizations a little while ago I mean the former "fake" private ones. This had been the case for Europe 1 whose stockholders are private, and this will be the case for a second peripheral station, Radio Monte Carlo, a large majority of which (83 percent) is held by Sofirad, a state organization—a subsidiary of the Treasury; and I could say the same for Sud-Radio. So, in principle, these two radio channels are going to be privatized, but no one, thank God, is dreaming of touching the public service radio, which seems to me absolutely essential, especially internationally. And I think that there is a fairly strong political consensus to provide the means for this radio to do its job. So, Radio France

Internationale, Radio France Outremer, specialized Radio France channels like France Musique or France Culture are not threatened. On the other hand, there have been changes within public radio. There have been many ideas from local public radio, radio solely for news, and there have been failures like Radio 7 in Paris. There have been these internal movements in public radio, but no one recommends privatization.

QUESTION: In France I believe there is a law, with no equivalent in the United States, concerning the rights of authors and their creations, which involves editing, especially in movies. An author can claim that his work has been distorted or oppose the cutting of two minutes to fit into time constraints. Will this cause problems for the new channels?

BARRET: It is true that there is a great difference in the United States and France in this situation. In the United States, for most audiovisual works, particularly the movies, the producer—the one who pays—has the final say on the material: its shape, presentation, and editing. The author has only the right, at this time, to remove his name, not to sign his name to the work in question. He who pays for it can modify it. In France the situation is completely different, for better or for worse. Authors have many of the most important rights, especially in the matter of final say. The producer cannot impose a new ending on his director, eliminate a passage, reduce a film's length, etc. These authors' rights have been reinforced over the past seven years, when Jack Lang was minister of culture. Clearly this subject has an affinity with a socialist political culture, but is also a result of strong lobbying by authors, and I am a party to that in another capacity.

However, in some situations this can become a bit dangerous because it leads to inflexibility. And the situation you mentioned in your question is one example. We today in France are on uncertain ground. In theory, no one can cut a film without the agreement of the director and the screenwriter; in practice, there are reasons to think that this will be handled with a bit of flexibility. Tensions in this area may be reduced because the candidates to be operators of the new channels have made extraordinarily precise agreements with representatives of the cinematographic industry.

This problem is more serious for the cinema than for work specifically created by television. In that case, circumstances are reversed: the producer has power over the author. Regarding films, those interested in operating the new channels could not become candidates until they had made these extremely constraining agreements with industry representatives. These potential candidates had to agree to show fewer films than are authorized for the public channels, for example, TF1. TF1 up to now showed 132 films per year, with some days completely forbidden: Wednesday, Friday night, Saturday, and Sunday before 8:30 P.M. This is to encourage people to go out, so they can watch movies in the theaters— so they won't be tempted to watch movies on TV. So, the movie industry had already lobbied and defended its turf; it started lobbying again with the privatizations, and succeeded much better than other businesses. For TF1, for example, I believe that Hachette has the same kind of agreement as did Bouygues: no more than 170 movies per year, of which only 140 can be shown in prime time, 8:30 in the evening, which is a small number. The effort these operators made is so great that the problem your question raised should not create major difficulties. Perhaps there will be a particular director who will object, but in general, things should go smoothly.

QUESTION: The French expect, I assume, that these new privatizations will provide a diversity of information. If the Hachette group is chosen, this pluralism is really in question. Isn't there a risk that the French will be disappointed and react to that?

BARRET: The expectations of the French in general is always a difficult subject. If you ask them what they want from television, they will say that they want programming much more cultural and educational than that shown today. And each time you put on such a program you lose about four-fifths of your audience. In reality, it is clear that far and away the most appealing programming is devoted to television series, with movies coming in a close second, then news.

In the matter of news, it is true that I believe that we must be careful and that too much concentrated power in any democracy is dangerous. The guarantee of pluralism is first of all pluralism of operators, the pluralism of publishers with different sensitivities; it is a series of simple, practical measures that result in a healthy situation. And it is true that France is somewhat threatened by not having pluralism in some cases. The commercial aspect of things can help. There was a good example of this in 1981 on FR3, France's third public TV channel. A particular news program had been especially militant for the new Socialist majority—this was around May or June of that year. When the next ratings came out, this program had slipped, for the French aren't fools. When they watch a program that calls itself a news program but which becomes too militant, they simply stop watching it and find something else more acceptable.

This economic rationale is not perfect, however, for there is the matter of news not totally or honestly provided: silence or manipulation. What concerns me is when private operators are too heavily dependent on public powers for their basic economic activities. Someone whose primary business is armaments, someone deeply involved in public works or state markets—one can always fear that such people might be tempted to be silent about disagreeable news concerning the government in power, to avoid making waves. I cannot speak about the Hachette group, but I know that in the candidature of Mr. Bouygues, there have been many organizational precautions taken to guarantee the editorial autonomy of TF1 should he be chosen.* I feel personally that there should be a system of barriers to allow editorial autonomy for TF1 and to minimize the opportunity for direct political pressure to be exerted.

---

*On 4 April 1987, the license for TF1 was awarded to a group headed by Francis Bouygues.

PART III

The Public Faces of
Business

I

The Business Press

Jean Boissonnat

There are three points that I wish to discuss concerning the business press in France. First, that it is exploding; second, that this explosion is the result of an evolution in thinking, which we will explore: this change in thinking is not simply in the French press, for the press has customers and reflects the evolution of its customers. Third, the evolution is also the result of a revolution that has affected the communication field in France. Thus, the business press is exploding because French thinking is evolving and the world of communications is experiencing a revolution.

HISTORICAL OVERVIEW

I should like to begin with some historical comments concerning the relationship between the business—or economic—world and communication.

We must remember that in France, the press was born from business activities. The French like to claim they invented the newspaper—the *Gazette* of Théophraste Renaudot, in the first half of the seventeenth century. In fact, this is untrue. All countries like to claim they are the first to have invented something, but we did not create the newspaper. Further, we should note that Renaudot's *Gazette* was overall the gazette of the Cardinal, Duc de Richelieu. He was writing under an assumed name in this paper to influence public opinion about his policies (We see that this is a long-lived practice!). And there were other newspapers in the sixteenth century as well.

I think the origin of the press can be found in confidential newsletters, the first of which originated in Augsbourg, a city dominated by the Fugger banking family. These first newsletters were called "Fuggers Zeitungen." The Fuggers used the network of their agents throughout the world as a source of information for the letters, which were written for "important" people, to inform them about events happening in the world. When we look at how the press was born, we find confidential newsletters, like those of the Fuggers, in Antwerp, Genoa, and Venice, all the large trading cities of the sixteenth century. Thus, there is, between the press and the business community something of a congenital alliance. News came from business, not business from news. Later, in the nineteenth century, press agencies arose from the need to inform the business world in industrial societies about he prices of raw materials and important political events, for example, the siege of Sebastopol, that influenced the course of business. So the press was really born from business and later from the development of stock exchanges: the need to publish figures. All of this helped shape journalistic life everywhere, including France, even if my country was not the most illustrious in these beginnings of the news media.

In the second place, as a result of the events of the 1930s, economics became the raw material of all news. It was no longer the private area of a business elite or specific, limited information on commodity prices or stockmarket value. Economics entered the general press because of economic and social spasms, the stockmarket crash, unemployment, devaluations of the 1930s, then, with World War II, rationing. At this time economics totally invaded the press because everyone (I was not very old then, but I remember very well) needed the newspapers to know which food tickets were needed to purchase items at the bakery, the butcher, and so forth.

After World War II a third event occurred: the big growth and modernization of the French economy; the ensuing development of the press was connected to this growth and modernization. The prewar press reflected the views of business people in the same way as Renaudot's *Gazette* expressed the point of view of Cardinal Richelieu. But at the end of the war, after the invasion of economic news in the general press, there progressively appeared a new wave of business press. This second generation of business press no longer reflected only the views of business circles, which in general speak only to themselves and do not generally attract followers. This second generation of the French business press can be found in publications like *l'Expansion* which I helped create exactly twenty years ago with Jean-Louis Servan-Schreiber (brother of Jean-Jacques, author of *Le défi americain*—"The American Challenge," and one of the founders of *l'Express*). "The American Challenge" introduced the concept of "managers" into France, that is, specialists in the management of businesses. The time of managers has passed, and today is the era of entrepreneurs. This is precisely one of the facets of French business affected by changes in thinking, as we shall see.

THE CURRENT FRENCH BUSINESS PRESS

The French business press can be divided into three categories: daily newspapers, weeklies, and monthlies and similar editions (see Exhibit 3).

Exhibit 3
The Business Press

Title	Type	Distribution	Advertising Revenue (000,000)
Les Echos	Daily	60,000	FF 140
La Tribune	Daily	35,000	43
L'AGEFI	Daily	7,000	52
La Cote Défossés	Daily	20,000	27
Le Monde	*	280,000	400
Le Figaro	*	450,000	280
Investir	Weekly	98,000	30
Journal des Finances	Weekly	55,000	35
La Vie Française	Weekly	112,000	74
Le Nouvel Economiste	Weekly	113,000	80
L'Usine Nouvelle	Weekly	60,000	--
Valeurs Actuelles	Weekly	85,000	33
L'Expansion	Bimonthly	160,000	142
Mieux Vivre	Monthly	77,000	11
Le Revenu Français	Monthly	115,000	11
L'Entreprise	Monthly	60,000	30
Science et Vie économie	Monthly	110,000	10

*Daily newspapers with business supplements.

Source: Author's figures, March 1987.

Dailies

There are four papers specifically devoted to business in France. *Les Echos* dates to the beginning of this century and was created, interestingly enough, by the Servan-Schreiber family, although not currently owned by it. Paid distribution is 60,000 (not including foreign distribution), and advertising revenues are currently FF 140 million. The second title is *La Tribune*, a successor of *Le Nouveau Journal*, itself a successor of *Les Informations*; so it is not really a new paper. *La Tribune* has an estimated domestic circulation of 35,000 and advertising revenues of FF 43 million.

The third daily has a very limited distribution, about 7,000, but it is quite prosperous because it appears in all financial organizations in France; reading it is obligatory. The paper is *Agefi* and belongs to the same publishing group as *La Tribune*. *Agefi* is a daily summary of what is published by the major press agencies, plus information from a worldwide network of correspondents. It is extremely useful: it is less expensive for a bank to subscribe to *Agefi* than to all the press agencies; further, it is well edited and easy to use. Advertising revenues amount to about FF 52 million.

The last title, *La Cote Défossés,* is one of two dailies (the other is *La Tribune*) that publish stockmarket results. The estimated distribution of this paper is 20,000, with modest advertising revenues of about FF 27 million. There are, however, two other sources of business news that are widely read: *Le Monde* (280,000 paid subscriptions, FF 400 million in advertising revenues); and *Le Figaro* (450,000 distribution, and about FF 280 million in advertising revenues, an estimation because weekend editions include magazines). These two daily newspapers have important business sections. The four dailies, however, that are specifically dedicated to business have a daily distribution of about 130,000, which is probably an overestimation.

Weeklies

There are two categories of weeklies: financial and economic. In the financial category, there is *Investir*, founded fifteen years ago, with a distribution of 98,000 and ad revenues of FF 30 million. The *Journal des Finances*, an independent magazine, has a distribution of 55,000 and ad revenues of FF 35 million. The largest distributed magazine, with 112,000, is *La Vie Française*, which belongs to the same group as *La Tribune* and *Agefi*; its advertising revenues are FF 74 million. All of these weekly magazines publish the stock market quotations.

In the economics category, we find magazines of a more general character that are not exclusively financial. There is *Le Nouvel Economiste*, the result of a merger of two older financial magazines; its distribution is 113,000, and ad revenues are currently about FF 80 million. *L'Usine Nouvelle* is concerned with technological matters and is read primarily by production engineers. Distribution is about 60,000 and I do not have a figure for its advertising revenues. Finally, there is *Valeurs Actuelles*, a magazine more political than the others, even if it bills itself as a business magazine. Its distribution is 85,000 and has advertising revenues of FF 33 million.

For France, these weeklies have a reasonable distribution level, about 100,000 apiece, but their advertising revenues remain rather modest; only *Les Echos*, a daily, has important advertising revenues.

Monthlies, etc.

I shall begin with *l'Expansion*, with all due modesty, which now appears bimonthly; originally it was monthly, but it evolved, like *Fortune*. I can verify our numbers: We have a distribution of 160,000 and advertising revenues of FF 142 million. In the monthly category there is *Mieux Vivre*, which concerns investments, and is roughly similar to the American magazine *Money*; its distribution is 77,000, and has modest advertising revenues of FF 11 million.

Then there is *Le Revenu Français*, a financial magazine with a consumer orientation, i.e., it is quite aggressive about different kinds of investments, not just those on the stock market; it addresses those who are interested in saving their money. Distribution is an honorable 115,000, but with its consumerist approach, it has small advertising revenues of FF 11 million.

L'Entreprise is a new monthly targeted to leaders of small and medium companies, and created by the Groupe Expansion, publishers of *l'Expansion*. It is practical, containing short articles devoted to financial and legal information, a bit like *Money* in the United States. We already have 60,000 subscribers and advertising revenue of FF 30 million, impressive figures for a magazine only two years old.

There are a few other titles that bear mentioning. *Science et Vie économique*, which appeared a few years ago, has an audience primarily of students. It uses an educational approach, with many graphs and drawings. Its distribution is 110,000, but, sadly, it has advertising revenues of only FF 10 million. The magazine is very interesting and generates young readers, giving them a taste of economics; I would hope that we would subsequently find them reading *l'Expansion* or *l'Entreprise*. *Tertiel*, which is somewhat like *l'Entreprise*, is addressed to young heads of business and was started by *l'Usine Nouvelle*, so its audience overlaps with it a bit; *Défi*, with a smaller circulation, once again similar to *l'Entreprise* but more for new entrepreneurs or company presidents. In other words, these magazines all reflect the evolution in thinking about which I would now like to speak.

What is interesting to see in the preceding analysis of the business press in France is that there are three families of publications: the older financial papers and magazines or the heirs to old titles; those that are about the general economy; and those addressing entrepreneurs. These three categories reflect the evolution of supply and demand in the world of economic data. In the past twenty years, the French have successively discovered the economy and its characteristics;

then business, and the reality of the marketplace, especially its connection to markets; and finally, the stock exchange, that is, plainly speaking, capitalism. Curiously, the oldest titles, although devoted to stockmarket information, have not followed the evolution in thinking; they continue to address the traditional stockmarket audience, ignoring the new clients of the market. The titles devoted to business were recently created when the French public discovered the business world. Finally, there are the general economic news titles, which reflect the French's discovery of the economy in the past twenty years.

CHANGING THINKING

What is this evolution in thinking? Why is there currently a need for both general and diversified economic information in the French society? I think several things have happened; I will review them rapidly. First was the crisis of the 1970s. Since 1973 the economic world was no longer a continuation of previous trends but became an unknown world: the oil crisis, the dollar crisis, the arrival of unemployment and new technologies. These awakened both curiosity and anxiety. And the only way to "manufacture" newspaper readers is to have both curiosity and anxiety: Anxiety without curiosity is only inhibition; curiosity without anxiety is only laziness. So, we had both curiosity and anxiety, the necessary components for generating readers.

The second factor in the last fifteen years is the decreasing role and influence of politics in France, particularly noticeable since the Left came to power. Until 1981, the French lived in fear of a Leftist government, thinking that the Left would change not only politics but society, not only the economy but the entire human race. When the Left did assume power in 1981, one year was enough for the Socialist government to discover the existence of the economy. It discovered that the balance of payments was difficult to circumvent; that businesses are a fact of life; that the economy will not prosper if businesses are going bankrupt; that unemployment existed and was resistant to rhetoric. Thus, after one year, in the summer of 1982, the Left began its big shift, and by the spring of 1983, one saw that the Left was no longer what it had been before. It discovered the Common Market, that it was necessary to remain within the European monetary system, and that belonging to this system meant adapting a certain type of economic policy and abandoning a certain kind of discourse.

We are lucky in France to be a medium-sized country, because when we make mistakes, we cannot make them very long. It is the great misfortune of the United States to be a large and powerful country: It can make mistakes for a long time. However, when the United States has to pay for these mistakes, it is very expensive. So, the French have this superiority over the United States, I modestly assert: We cannot make mistakes for a very long time. We experienced this when the Left took power. Then, politics stopped being interesting. The French— who for the past two centuries have spent their time imitating the French Revolution and have a permanent need for a political theater that mimics the Revolution, creates Dantons and Robespierres, and, therefore, Louis XVI, so his head can be cut off—found a substitute for Louis XVI in the constitution of the Fifth Republic. That is, it is the constitution of a monarchist republic, and every seven years the monarch's head is cut off, but without a drop of bloodshed. This is the ideal system for the French, a people of regicides. Thanks to the constitution of the Fifth Republic, a purely monarchist constitution, we can cut the king's head off without having a revolution. I think, from a political point of view—economic and social as well—our present system is the best and important to keep; moreover, I notice that no one wants to change it.

Today, politics have less appeal for people because the different options are similar. A good example is an article *l'Expansion* recently published that was a face-to-face meeting between Mr. Michel Rocard and Mr. Raymond Barre, two men who surely will be running for president. You can find striking convergences between them on very important topics.

Thus, French political life has become ordinary, and because modern societies need entertainment, the drama has moved from politics to economics. The truth of this statement can be found in the fact that business people have become stars of the media. The biggest star of French public life today is Bernard Tapie. Mr. Tapie has yet to buy anything in the United States, but that will come. He attracts overflow crowds of the young, saddens the old, worries bankers, fascinates television, and dominates newspapers. An interview with Bernard Tapie will double your sales. The same is true for Mr. Francis Bouygues, who is in the construction business. The speciality of Mr. Tapie is purchasing dying businesses, preferably those already dead, because that allows him to lay off employees without asking for authorization and without having to pay off the business' debts. Mr. Bouygues has undertaken some of the most beautiful projects in the world, with the company bearing his name. He currently is a candidate for ownership of a French television channel. Then there is Mr. Jean-Luc Lagardère, surely another candidate for purchasing the TV channel, as he and Mr. Bouygues are competitors; both of them also manufacture military missiles, specifically the Exocet missle.

So, the great stars of French public life today are businessmen, no longer politicians. On the other hand, we can say that the great events are of an economic character even in politics. The great change in the Left's legislative policy came in 1983 when President Mitterrand chose to stay in the European Monetary System; all that followed was a result of that decision. In the same way, the new liberal majority that recently came to power has distinguished itself by privatizations; it is nearly the only thing that this majority can show as an uncontested success.

Economics, then, has become a substitute for politics. And there has also been an evolution in attitudes, and on this point I would like to mention some results of a poll we published in *l'Expansion* in 1986. These clearly reveal changes in young people's attitudes toward money. I shall cite a few questions, especially the first: "When you are told about someone who made a fortune in a few years, do you feel admiration or distrust about this person?'' In 1984 the results for this same question were: admiration, 34 percent; distrust, 47 percent. Two years later—not twenty, only two—for the same question: admiration 43 percent; distrust 42 percent. Thus, in two years we moved from a negative balance of thirteen points to a positive balance of one point. If these results are examined by socioprofessional categories, by age group, and political preferences, two things appear. The social categories that most admire those who made a fortune within a few years (and this is fundamental, as a signpost of the future) are two: women and young people. Regarding the age groups: In the category of ages eighteen to twenty-four, 52 percent feel admiration, in contrast to an overall 43 percent; in the group above sixty-five, only 23 percent feel admiration. Thus, there are twice as many young people who feel admiration. The results are the same for women: 45 percent of the women feel admiration against 40 percent of the men. Here again we have an essential difference that is a portent of the future.

Another question shows the evolution in thinking. "Do you consider money, in today's society, a positive or negative thing?'' This question is about money, not success. Money is something in this old, rural, and Catholic society, the French civilization, that has numerous bad connotations—many papers have been written on this topic. In fact, 71 percent of the respondents think of money as something positive, and only 21 percent as negative. Considering these results according to political preference, members of the French Communist Party, people whom one would expect to be less in favor of money, were 53 percent positive about money; only 33 percent said money is negative.

A final question to show changes in thinking concerns a moral judgment about investment. "Here are different ways of spending a million francs. From a moral point of view, would you agree with spending money this way—totally or not at all? That is, do you entirely agree with spending money on this or not at all? The top of the approval list for spending money completely was, not surprisingly, in the purchase of housing. Ninety-three percent of the respondents think it is moral to spend one million francs to buy an apartment (which, of course, in Paris is a studio). Other options presented were "to buy gold'' (and the French have a long fascination with gold), "to invest in the stock market,'' "to spend it,'' "to save in case of need,'' "to buy an aparatment not for yourself but to lease it,'' "to start a business,'' and so forth.

What came in second? In second, 74 percent of the answers were "to create an enterprise.'' Of course they would not do so, thank God for them because a lot would lose their money. But this shows how those who do start businesses are regarded by the French: If they had a million francs this is what they would dream about. Put another way, to start a business is not necessarily the goal of the French, but it is their dream, and their dream is more important than the goal.

Between investing in stocks or purchasing gold, the traditional choice would be gold. The old French are not interested in paper, they prefer what is material.

Yet 35 percent of the poll's respondents would buy gold and 52 percent would invest in stock; that is a change in thinking.

I would like to mention some other numbers based not on opinion but on facts. There is a survey run by INSEE (National Institute for Statistics and Economics Studies) that is published several times a year. It contains a question similar to the one just discussed: "If you suddenly received a big sum of money, what would you do with it?" In the beginning of 1984, 7.5 percent indicated they would buy stock and 7 percent would buy gold. In late 1986, the last known results, 13 percent would buy stocks, and only 5 percent would buy gold. In other words, today, three times more people would buy stocks than gold. As proof of that, in the past five years, the value of stocks in France has multiplied by four. Here, then, is the evolution of demand.

SUPPLY AND DEMAND

Facing the evolution of demand we have an evolution of supply which is in part deduced from the demand. But the supply is evolving in different ways. We have seen the arrival of new magazines and newspapers and their variety, especially a business press that did not previously exist—that is, one directed to entrepreneurs. We also see economic issues addressed in the general press. *Le Figaro* publishes an economic supplement each Monday; *Le Monde* publishes an economic supplement each Friday. Take a newspaper like *Libération*, which today is quite fashionable—if you want to be "in" and completely detached from the world of money. Well, for a year, *Libération* has published excerpts from the stock exchange. Completely unimaginable for Jean-Paul Sartre, the intellectual founding father of this paper. If today he could see his offspring publishing stockmarket reports in his paper, he would turn over in his grave. And what would Stalin say if he could see the central organ of the Italian Communist Party? For over a year, *l'Unità* has published stockmarket reports. All the Latin countries are in the process of modifying their relations with money.

Thus, there has been an evolution of supply that is not simply the result of the evolution of demand but is connected to deep structural changes in the world of French communication and education.

The sudden arrival of five general television channels plus one pay channel—six in all—will of course change the advertising market, which is different in France from what it is elsewhere, and press groups are reacting to this phenomenon in different ways. First, they are trying to multiply the number of specialized publications. Television is a mass tool; that is, it addresses people in general without selecting them, even if some can be selected depending on the time period. Thus, if you want to retain a piece of the advertising pie, you must develop specialized publications, particularly for the economic press. So, as I mentioned, we have the Hersant group and its *Le Figaro* with the economic supplement; there is the Goldsmith group that publishes *l'Express* and an economics supplement; the Hachette group (the Lagardère group) is preparing an economics magazine for students. There is everywhere the need not only to satisfy the demand I earlier described, but to retain the advertising market. This market can swing toward television brutally—in a matter of weeks or months; television supported by advertising is now installed in the communication world of France.

Another element modifying supply is, as I mentioned, privatization: The number of stockholders has already doubled in France. Today there are around 3 million stockholders; there were 1.5 million one year ago. Three million is not a lot for a total population of 55 million, in comparison with the United States, which has 60 million stockholders; but it's a lot more than before. And we will see a new form of institutional advertising. Companies will be coming on the market with numerous stockholders, some of whom will be intently curious about the evolution of their stock. For example, the *Expansion* group is very democratic and socially oriented—i.e., we are not against trade unions, all of which can express themselves; we have representatives of all unions. However, there are more members in the stockholders club for the *Expansion* company than there are members of unions in the company . . . an interesting anecdote that illustrates this evolution of public taste.

So, there will be new kind of publicity developed: institutional advertising. Naturally, the economic and financial media are a welcoming environment for this development. In addition, publicity for new financial products—notably the capitalized retirement plan—will be created in France. Thus, advertising in business newspapers is not much; if I isolated from all advertising that which is solely financial, that too would not be very much. We see emerging a new development that explains the evolution of supply.

CONCLUSION

Having presented the basic elements of the development of the business press in France, I would like to conclude with some general remarks. The business press will grow, but it must evolve in style and structure. We at *l'Expansion* are running some surveys and are very careful to follow the evolution of our readers. We regularly force ourselves to change the structure of our publication to conform to an audience that we recognize is in full evolution. We must apply to ourselves what we say in our articles. We observe that our own readers are changing their habits of reading because of the role television plays in their access to information. We have to create a kind of writing that is adapted to this new kind of reading. Here in the United States there is a newspaper—*USA Today*—which has articles that are very short, the title is self-explanatory, the texts are not linked, but the paragraphs are placed side by side in a way that you can perceive them like a drawing, not the way you do in reading. The eye is reading the paper, not the brain. The brain reads, I would say, afterwards. Thus, we have to work very hard in the economic and financial press to adapt to a public that is "deformed." Whether this is good or bad is not our problem.

Our customers are deformed by watching television. We must provide them a vehicle in which the writing corresponds to this distortion. They are reading differently.

In addition, the economist—that is, the expert who speaks *ex cathedra*, pouring his knowledge all over the reader—has lost some of his luster. After fifteen years of economic crises, the expert has not resolved the problem of unemployment. We continue to listen, but we do not want him telling us too much. We want him to address us with less arrogance, less *hubris*. The expert knows things we don't, so we want to interrogate him, but he is not entitled to deliver sermons. So, in this area, we have to express things differently. He is still a magician, but he is losing some of his knack, and he must be aware of his reader's new orientation.

Another element we observe in the evolution of our customers is the concept of "le cadre"—the upper level supervisory employee—which had been at the origin of the modern economic press, notably at the birth of *l'Expansion*. When we were born in 1977, we focused on the myth of "le cadre." Well, this myth has been overexploited in the past twenty years and has now become common-place. Today we have to speak to someone who is entrepreneurial; he is not necessarily an entrepreneur, but he is entrepreneurial. In other words, someone who seeks hope in economic life. If we are always saying: "The dollar is going to fall; it's the end of the world; the underdeveloped countries are going bankrupt; unemployment will only rise; inflation is low today but it will take off again tomorrow; interest rates are a bit lower today but this won't last''; then the budget deficit will never be resolved. If we use this so-called demystifying language of economic reality, we are using a hopeless language. Our reader wants us to tell him the truth—we cannot tell him that the dollar is rising when it is falling, and in all cases, if it rises or falls, it is never good. But we must tell him: "Well, in this difficult economic life there are reasons for hope. There are those who make it; there are successful countries; there are unemployment rates that fall; some currencies are stabilized. And for you in your business, there are companies that resolve their problems, who find new products and markets." We have a readership that demands more optimism from the economic press. And I believe that is something very important for our evolution.

Finally, there is diversification. We no longer have only one economic press but many. Not only the financial press, the general economic press, the business press, the service press—but by stratum of customers: top level customers who are reached, for example, by newsletters. In our group we have three newsletters: one daily, two weekly—one having a general approach, the other more oriented toward the social management of companies. For another kind of customer it will be necessary to use an electronic mail system. For another we need colorful magazines; for another we must devise dailies that are easy to read, with quick access. We need to diversify, to divide the world of the economic press into subgroups.

And what could interfere with the continued progress of the business press in

France? Several things. A crash of the financial system. Do not be surprised if from time to time we inquire about the behavior of American political and monetary authorities. A reverse in the Bourse could cause the French to rediscover their reflexes of the beginning of the eighteenth century and Mr. Law. Under the pretext of discovering America, Mr. Law drained people's savings and threw them into the ocean . . . and the Russian loans . . . everything the entire French population learned in elementary school. We do not need a very big crash of the Bourse, for many stockholders are beginners and they imagine the Bourse to be a casino in which all the numbers are winners, which obviously isn't true. And it would not be helpful if our new business stars begin to weaken. If the businesses of Messrs. Tapie, Bouygues, and Lagardère and others suddenly fell apart, that surely would have consequences. The business press would not disappear because the fundamental reasons for its existence are of another nature. But such things would impede its development or jeopardize it. Ultimately, the business press is a way of looking at the totality of the French society from a particular point of view.

DIALOGUE

QUESTION: Regarding your statement that the second thing someone in France would do with his or her money would be to start a business: We have heard that the difficulties in doing so are almost impossible to overcome. How do you reconcile these two points of view?

BOISSONNAT: Recall what I said before: It is a dream of the French, not necessarily a goal. No policy can prevent you from dreaming. The most negative policy is the best for keeping the dream alive, for that way the dream cannot become a reality. It ensures the dream's longevity. But this is intangible. I think you are right and your information is correct. French legislation has not been created to encourage the development of young entrepreneurs. However, some things are changing. One example is the secondary market at the Paris Bourse. A company can go into this market even with a rather low volume of business and it can put up only 10 percent of its capital; to enter the main market on the Bourse, a company must put up 25 percent of its capital.

There are also future prospects. Today more than 200 companies are rated on this secondary market, and only 500 are on the first market, so there is a high speed of growth here. Also, over the past twenty years, the number of companies rated on the first market has dropped to 500 from 1,000 for a variety of reasons that do not concern us here. Therefore, in my view, the secondary market will be a stong incentive for business creation because it is what allows a young entrepreneur or someone who becomes an entrepreneur in the course of his career to tell himself that he had a chance to succeed, if he has been successful.

One cannot make a fortune with the French tax system, and the system will not be changed tomorrow morning because to change it you have to accept a decrease in revenues, which means accepting lower expenditures. So the French tax revolution will not be very swift. It would be unthinkable in France to enact the tax reform that you have had in the United States. Your businesses' social costs are only 30 percent, whereas they are 45 percent in France. Which means you have to cut into the flesh. On the other hand, this can allow a tax reform that weighs heavily on business but is beneficial to individuals. This is very schematic, and things are a lot more complicated. The current state of French business does not permit additional burdens; in fact, it is necessary to ease their tax burdens, and it would be better to increase taxes at the individual level. In France, 10 million people do not pay income taxes. Among the advanced industrialized countries, we have the fewest people paying income taxes. Thus, someone starting his own business says to himself: "So, if I am successful, when I am forty or forty-five years old, I will be able to recoup my investment because I will have a capital gain. This is because I will no longer have a salary which is . . . " Of course, when he reaches a high enough level, he is taxed at 50 percent or more. Thus, the expectation of sweating your shirt off during ten years to create a business and then to be taxed more than 50 percent a year is not elating. With the secondary market, however, you put your company on the stock market and eventually you can sell it to someone at a certain price, for you will have had a market listing.

QUESTION: I am astonished by the way French reporters ask questions of a president whose company is being introduced onto the Bourse, to an American reporter asking similar questions to an executive of an American company whose company is also put on the stock market. It seems to me that there is a code of ethics specific to business reporters that differs from that of traditional reporters. What kind of rules do you think are relevant in this area to avoid stock-market manipulation at the news level? What kind of rules would you see given to a business or economic reporter?

BOISSONNAT: First, I don't know that there aren't kinds of information that can manipulate stock-market prices in America; there has been news of that recently. I would like to believe that no American reporter was involved in such leaking of information but . . . In fact, we must be self-critical in our profession. Journalists who specialize in French economic life are more numerous and better trained than they were twenty years ago, but they still do not have the skill level of many of their foreign colleagues. We must face that fact so we can work to improve. Oddly, financial mechanisms are not part of their education; frequently, they are reasonably learned about general economics and industrial economics. But they are still weak in financial matters. Thus, reporters who begin to interrogate a head of a company that has just gone onto the Bourse do not always have sufficient training to ask the pertinent questions. And I might add in their defense that they are facing people who try to direct their thinking, and this does not ease the journalists' task. Naturally, there are exceptions. After all, we cannot resent a CEO who presents his activities positively. So, a reporter should be well equipped to be aware of a natural manipulation on the part of his interviewee. There is some training that can be done in schools, but overall, this must be done on the job—to learn a company's real situation from a financial point of view.

I have a short story that occurred recently in my press group. We were in an editorial meeting, exchanging information about ongoing investigations—we take great pains in these company inquiries, for example, of Schlumberger, Renault, Bouygues, Matra. A reporter will often spend two months, meeting fifty people, and so forth. In this editorial meeting, however, we noticed that there was something missing from information about a company: its *fiche d'identité boursière*, or financial report. We had no information about price-earnings ratio, about the evolution of its stock on the market, anything about the opinions of financial analysts, as if this were not our world. We, who have the best economic journal in France, with the best articles on business—we said nothing about this aspect of things. So, we have imposed on ourselves the same method one would use with a country: You show a map, indicating where the country is. Brazil, for example. The French don't know their geography, so you must tell them where Brazil is. In the same way, you tell them where Schlumberger is on the financial market, where Bouygues is, or Matra. Even if this isn't the principal object, you must provide a financial "identity card."

The point here is that our education, our natural curiosity, lags behind reality. I don't want to imply that financial information should obscure the rest. I also wish that French reporters keep their reflexes, that they go to see what a manufacturing plant is, that they discuss with marketing people, that they are not content only with financial analyses. But without a doubt, we are slow in this area.

Another major backwardness concerns writing. As I mentioned, our writing style in the economic press was becoming too obscure, too heavy, for a large audience, an audience biased by TV watching, for better or for worse.

2

The Evolution of Corporate Relations

Jean-Pierre Beaudoin

The French, traditionally considered financially immature and reluctantly European, have recently shown a capacity to integrate two new perspectives into their daily opinion-forming process; this reveals how deep the evolution has penetrated. First has been the tidal wave of stock purchases by small investors in privatized companies, along with the absence of a reverse movement when prices collapsed in the fall of 1987. Second is the general awareness of 1992. This has been an omnipresent political issue and a part of corporate communications. For the French public, these two new perspectives are more than a media-created fad. Both reveal a deep change in the general frame of reference, and both modify the context and responsibilities of corporate communications.

CORPORATE CHAMPIONS IN A EURO-TEAM

That the French have placed their hope in corporations transcends a disappointment with government policies that have failed to fight rising unemployment and that risk reducing purchasing power. The new attraction the French have toward business is the result of longstanding educational efforts by both public and private organizations. Today, most media have economic and business sections, if not weekly supplements; stock exchange reports on electronic media, if not as numerous or yet as popular as weather forecasts, bring thrills to large sections of the public. In addition, of course, the widely reported and applauded rise in stock prices over recent years has greatly contributed to attracting individual investors. But even if the multiplication of small investors was a result of wanting to become small profiteers rather than a sudden sense of national support for our gallant fighters in world competition, it nonetheless has made new investors pay more attention to business.

Overall, the French have now acquired some understanding and appreciation of profit and taken the measure of international competition. Resistance to the dismantling of outdated, overweight sectors, such as those found in the mining, steel, textile, shipbuilding, and automotive industries, has finally broken down. As a result, France is viewed as part of a European ensemble, and French companies are seen as one component of a European force vis-à-vis other regions of the world. France is less to be considered as "France Against the World"; rather, the role of French business in Europe is to make French companies European leaders in world competition.

Another factor in this changing perspective is generational. Corporate, public, and political leaders until recently have been from a generation that grew up in the Second World War and whose perspective was primarily national. Today, those taking charge are people in their early forties, who were born in the postwar period and grew up in the construction of Europe. They have learned a different history, learned geography by traveling, and more of them than is assumed have learned to express themselves in more than one language. As usual, those living in the present world are the successors of those that shaped it.

FROM DREAMS TO EXPECTATIONS TO DEMANDS

The great Gaullist dream of popular capitalism began to become a reality through the Chiraquian privatization program, thanks to the socialist-communist nationalization program of seven years ago. Hence, even if not willingly, nearly all political "families" will have contributed to achieving a project that seemed inevitably to be a dream. History has thus forced its way through. But the Gaullist concept of participation meant more than just ownership. The mobilization effort that advertising mounted during the privatization period was geared mostly toward securing investors, thus creating ownership by giving the illusion of participation. If one was one of the happy few (eventually numbering in millions), one received personal letters from famous CEOs of no less famous companies, presenting details of intimate corporate strategy. Company advertisements, brochures, telephone and electronic services provided a direct access to wealth— or corporate information and answers to personal questions. And if one was wise enough to buy shares, one even got to meet top management at stockholders' meetings.

Now is the time for expectations. This means dividends, of course, and continued appreciation of stock prices. It also means a continued association with the life of a company in which one has a stake, however small. This is all the more true for company employees. Failing to meet financial expectations may not be a company's fault; failing to meet communication expectations, however, would. Already, organized groups of new stockholders are demanding information, and keeping them as stockholders is a matter of corporate will. This, along with the integration of a European dimension into the way the French perceive themselves and the world, gives business new responsibilities.

The latest "Eurobarometer," an opinion survey of citizens in all twelve EEC member countries, shows that the French are among the most positive toward the post-1992 challenge, a result that is reinforced when the upper and younger classes are considered. For example, a survey made by a trade union confirms that over 70 percent of French corporate managers consider the unification of the European market an opportunity. Nevertheless, a distinction must be made between overall attitude and personal position. If people from the higher ranks of corporate hierarchies are motivated by the challenge, individual employees show signs of uncertainty about the fate of their employers, thus their jobs, when faced with more open competition. Thus, another corporate responsibility is to state clearly to employees how the company is preparing for 1992 and how this will affect its development.

Likewise, the European component of a company's image is strengthening in corporate communication. A company taking a defensive stance or seeming to demand protection against increased competition will be perceived as backward-looking, fragile, and untrustworthy, and this will have consequences for many aspects of corporate life.

MARIANNE IN A GREY FLANNEL SUIT

In every city hall in France is a bust of Marianne, who personifies the Republic (similar to Uncle Sam in the United States). Since the 1880s, Marianne has been depicted as a motherly lady; in the 1960s she took on the characteristics of a seductive younger woman. Today, however, Marianne wants to present herself more like a corporate executive than a protective mother or a gratifying mate.

The state, of course, still causes the greatest changes in French perceptions of business: The state decides to continue with European unification; the state decides to privatize major companies. But it is less and less the state that tells individual companies—as was the case not too long ago—where to invest, at what price to sell products, or what wages to pay employees. The state has even stopped subsidizing ailing firms with no clear future, the so-called lame ducks, and interfering with mergers, acquisitions, and takeover attempts when they represent no breach of law. There are, however, persistent exceptions to this new approach.

Here again, public opinion has evolved. Not long ago, corporate strategies included systematic appeals to public authorities, from whom decisions, incentives, and pressures were demanded. Trade unions would make demands when jobs were at stake; corporate management would make demands when financial support of foreign market penetration was desired. These demands became political issues, for the government in power was blamed for layoffs, and ministers were the first to boast of their role in securing large export contracts. Now, however, corporate responsibilities are more clearly in the hands of management, and public opinion looks favorably on responsible companies; it would distrust management calling for government assistance. And corporate communication strategies fully acknowledge this change in public opinion; any state intervention in the affairs of individual corporations tends to be viewed as an abuse.

Thus, Marianne, the personification of the Republic, is a partner of business, not a substitute for weak management. As a result, in a growing number of companies, the "public affairs" function has emerged. Companies and trade organizations recognize they must explain their strategies, objectives, and policies to government authorities, so that these will be taken into account when legislation or regulations are being debated or international negotiations undertaken. Companies realize that they should no longer, or less systematically, expect public authorities to manage in their place.

Simultaneously, enforcement of the 1982 decentralization law has endowed regional and local governments with responsibilities previously held by the central government, so the range of public partners for corporate communications has consequently expanded. And it is no longer sufficient for a corporate head only to have been in the same grande école with a fair number of high ranking civil servants to ensure appropriate relations with government. Though, of course, this never hurts.

WILL IT LAST?

With such a major evolution underway, corporate relations in France will continue to become more professional. Not only will they assume a more appropriate place within companies, they will better integrate financial communications, the European dimension, and enable more orderly government relations.

Evolutions, however, can change direction, but returning to a domestic- and government-centered pattern is both unlikely and impractical. Financial and cooperative agreements with other European countries have become commonplace. France, whose country is half northern and half southern, sees the benefits of arrangements like the Airbus consortium. It has become familiar with business leaders who have names like Sir Jimmy Goldsmith and Carlo De Benedetti. In fact, the French public has begun to realize that these are names of European business leaders and that the others, the non-Europeans, are more alien.

The French are traditionally described as chauvinistic and protectionist. It would be ironic, should France's recent appreciation for business competitiveness and the European challenge be confirmed, if this country proves the quickest to adjust to the necessary transcultural thinking among European nations.

3

The French Style of Advertising

Claude Marcus

The French are often accused of arrogance, and I wouldn't want to give credence to this stereotype by my title, *The French Style of Advertising*. We recognize in France, perhaps more than in any other country, that practically all the techniques of modern advertising were invented in the United States. But, if you watch television commercials, you will see that there is a difference between those that you see here and the ones produced in France. The difference is in style; if bouillabaisse is different from clam chowder, it doesn't mean that one is better than the other; they are just two different styles of cooking. I will try to point out what differences create our style by showing you examples of current French advertising.

Before talking about advertising today, however, I would like to give you some background information, both qualitative and quantitative, that will point out the particularities of the French situation. My presentation is as much about specificity, perhaps, as about style. The evolution of advertising in my country explains why our advertising is different today from yours.

First, the qualitative aspect: Traditionally the French have not liked advertising. *The French Do Not Like Advertising* was, in fact, the title of a popular book written thirty years ago. A few years ago, the National Organization of French Advertising Companies ran a survey that revealed two totally distinct reactions to advertising. On the one hand, people claimed that they did not like advertising; on the other, when they were asked about DIM's hosiery commercials, they replied: "Oh magnificent! They're beautiful!" This double reaction is typical; it is almost a national characteristic of the French to have such a reaction. The French may be Socialists, but they protest against taxes. We have generous ideals but, day to day, we are just like everyone else. At any rate, although the French have begun to change their attitude to advertising (as the figures given below indicate), the fact that we in ad agencies have lived for many years in a hostile environment has affected the way advertising has evolved.

Continuing with the quantitative background information, we can say that from an economic point of view advertising is doing quite well in France. Revenues have risen about 14 percent per year since 1981, with a low inflation rate. On the other hand, investment in French advertising is lower than what is invested in large western countries, in relative as well as absolute terms. In France, 0.9 percent of the GNP is invested in advertising, whereas that figure is over 2 percent in the United States, a country with a GNP fourteen times that of France.

The breakdown among the different media in France differs from that in the United States. The press dominates the French advertising landscape with 58 percent of revenues; next comes television with 19 percent, and the third is outdoor advertising with 13 percent. Radio accounts for only 8.5 percent of advertising revenues; cinema is 1.5 percent, a low percentage, but certainly more than in the United States where it is almost nonexistent. These statistics, which will probably be affected in the near future by the privatization of French television channels, call for a number of remarks.

From 1947 to 1981, French political policy, regardless of the party in power, protected the press by forbidding advertising on television and radio. Advertising is still not allowed on public radio stations. The 8.5 percent of total advertising revenues attributed to radio in the figures given above comes from the peripheral radio stations: Radio Luxembourg, Europe 1, Radio Monte Carlo, and Sud-Radio. These stations broadcast on long wave and cover three-quarters of French territory. The stations' principal studios are in Paris, although their transmitters are beyond French borders. Further, the French government is the majority shareholder of Radio Monte Carlo and Europe 1 and holds considerable shares in Radio Luxembourg. Thus, although advertising is forbidden on public radio, the government is actually the owner of stations that advertise. In recent years, another phenomenon has appeared: "free radio," which are local stations that transmit on FM. There are several hundred of these, authorized by the Mitterrand government, beginning in 1981. Government authorized these radio stations but, originally, forbade their source of financing—advertising. People recognized the absurdity of this. It would be difficult to authorize a retail business yet forbid it to sell. So, advertising on local private radio stations was allowed in 1984.

Advertising was not permitted on television either until 1968, and then only agricultural products, consumer associations, and the like could advertise, not brand names. The doors were opened subsequently, but not completely, for two reasons. First, on public television channels (private channels are only in the process of appearing) the total volume of advertising is fixed by law each year, and is about 60 percent to 70 percent of what could be supplied if permitted. Secondly, some economic sectors, such as retailing, tourism, computers, and publishing, cannot advertise on television. The rationale for this is not only to protect the press, but to protect small business.

I should mention also that France is probably the last and only country where radio is not locally supported (with the exception of the "free" radio), and local television has existed for only a short time. Since we have attempted to regionalize advertising only recently, we suffer from a shortage of local media. Small firms have suffered since they do not have the funds to advertise nationally and lack the means of broadcasting their message locally.

Another consequence of insufficient television time (this may change with the upcoming privatizations) is the surprising 15.5 percent of all advertising devoted to public displays, such as posters and billboards. Americans seem just recently to have found out about the effectiveness of the complementarity of television and public display, something that has been known and used in France for some time. We have also discovered the use of advertising in bus shelters. A man named Decaux went all through France equipping cities and towns with small bus shelters; in exchange, he was granted a license to display advertising on them for a certain number of years. Because these shelters are in downtown areas, are well lighted and well maintained, and the advertising displays change every eight days, they have become an extraordinary medium. Consequently, because of this competition, other companies have upgraded their billboards, lighting, and maintenance. This accounts for the high percentage of advertising in the form of public display in France.

Another aspect of the specificity of French advertising is its reliance on cinema. In Europe, especially in France, commercials are shown in movie theaters before the main feature. In the beginning, these advertising films were mediocre, but they have become beautiful examples of cinematography. This is a remarkable medium because it hits a very precise target audience, the fourteen- to twenty-eight-year-old age group. The market share attributed to cinema, 1.5 percent of total advertising revenues, may seem small, but this is because the audience in movie theaters is limited, never more than 180 million spectators altogether per year, as compared to 20 or 30 million in front of the television every evening. But research has shown that cinema advertising reaches the public in a different way. Cinema obtains memorization coefficients six times superior to those of television. So we have less impact numerically, but a fantastic qualitative impact; the audience is captivated by the images of the wide screen.

The public's reaction today to cinema advertising is indicative of the change in mentality. Originally, when commercials were shown in movie theaters, people would leave their seats, talk or eat candy (not popcorn, there is no popcorn in France!). Today, people not only watch the commercials, they listen to them and talk about them. This new attitude appeared in about 1983, at about the same time as the French started liking business.

Advertising, then, has developed differently in France from the way it has evolved in the United States. French advertisers have had a difficult time, on the one hand, because the population is basically antagonistic to advertising and, on the other, because they have not always been free legally to do whatever they wanted. The second problem could be tackled directly, by dealing with the government, and we have seen some changes—more advertising on television and radio, as I have pointed out. The first problem, however, changing a mindset, was more difficult. So, what did we do? We had to coat the pill and make advertising more appealing, and the ways to do that were to utilize either sensuality, humor, or spectacular effects.

Essentially, the difference between French and American advertising is that we consistently avoid the hard sell, which has short-term objectives, and concentrate on the long term. We feel that the hard sell can destroy a product in very sensitive markets, like fashion or perfume. Our advertising is directed to the senses, with more attention paid to visual and auditory stimuli. We are not trying to create a conviction, but an impression that appeals to the emotions.

We believe more in the power of pictures, of images, than in the power of words. In fact, sometimes the soundtrack of our advertising films contains only a brief dialogue, or none at all. We believe that you can imply quality by the quality of the communication without saying "We are good." We don't believe in the kind of advertising showing a family around a breakfast table drinking coffee and marveling at how good it is.

On the other hand, I would say that we use music consistently, almost as a musical logo; for us, music is always one of the elements of the message, often more important than words. For example, in 1970, when my agency first started creating the DIM stocking commercials, we used music from an American film called *The Fox*. This music caught on and we have used it in all the DIM commercials all over Europe ever since. More recently, South American music that we adapted for a film about Nescafé became so popular that we sold 800,000 records: sold, not gave away. This music is now used in all Nescafé commercials. In the case of Maggi, a company that had an old-fashioned image, we decided to do a series of films based on a big musical show. We asked Serge Gainsbourg, a well-known French singer, to help us with the music. As a result, the company has been turned around, and half of France started singing *Maggi*.

French advertising agencies not only have their music written by established composers, they use well-known film directors also. Jean-Jacques Annaud, who made *The Name of the Rose,* has worked with us for fifteen years. Many others—including Sergio Leone, William Klein, Hugh Hudson, Costa Gavras, and Diane Kurys—are working with us and they like it. This is probably one of the reasons for the quality of our productions. The cost of a film is such that it justifies working with the best talent available.

Another significant difference, which is one of attitude perhaps, rather than style, is that we sign our advertising. I think France is the only country in the world where agencies put their name on the advertising they produce regardless of the medium: in the press, posters, or film. This is significant for two reasons: First, our signature shows that we are proud of what we do, and secondly, we openly accept our responsibility toward the public.

Having now spent all this time talking about the specificity of French advertising—its particular history and characteristics—I would also like to explain that French style is not necessarily exclusively French. For example, a commercial can be of French style if it is made in France by the French branch of an American agency for an American product. This is similar to the way in which foreign artists, such as Soutine or Modigliani, were considered to belong to the "Ecole de Paris" because they were influenced by their Parisian environment, and the friends, clients, critics, and galleries with whom they worked.

Paradoxically, advertising is perhaps the most international of fields, while remaining essentially country based. Competitors are worldwide, as are clients and their customers. Is it "French" or "American" when General Foods discusses advertising with its agency in Paris? In fact, as suggested above, American advertising in France is partly French, and advertising of French products in the United States is American. Although the methods will be those of the parent company, the local culture will be present and expressed. If we were to watch a randomly selected commercial in Europe, without hearing the language, we could immediately distinguish a German from an English, French, or Italian advertisement. This means that creating a commercial that will work the world over is difficult, but not impossible. When an advertisement works well in one market, it can always be tested elsewhere. And if it works, you are on the way to a global commercial.

DIALOGUE

QUESTION: Do you think the French style of advertising would work in America? I know that our commercials are aimed at the consumer who is not paying attention, who gets up during the commercial to get something from the kitchen. Do you see, any time in the future, that we will have the quality of advertising that you have in France?

MARCUS: I can't really answer your question. I know that I see more and more advertising in America that is of the same level of quality, such as Apple, General Electric, or Pepsi Cola. I've seen here some remarkable, funny, or beautiful films. But it's true that it takes not only the talent, which you obviously have in this country, but also client attitude that will accept that sort of film. I'm convinced that the American advertising has suffered from an excess of research that kills a lot of potentially very good advertising. Of course we need research, but it's not the answer to everything. When you test nonconventional advertising, it is likely to be rejected because people are disturbed by what is new, whether it is art or advertising. It takes time for people to get used to innovation, but testing cannot include the time dimension. Picasso's paintings, Christian Dior's "new look", or the Guggenheim Museum would certainly have been rejected if they had been tested.

QUESTION: One of the hallmarks of French advertising in the cinema has always been two- or three-minute films, but the commercials you showed today were only twenty or forty-five seconds long. Is there a decrease in the length that the advertisers want or that the public will accept now?

MARCUS: Length is a question of frequency and money. Usually, we'd like to have longer films. Not too long, but we prefer a thirty-second to a fifteen-second film. We have a 45-second version of the EuropAssistance film that you saw today, and a thirty-second version. This year we are running a 20-second version, because when people have the longer film, the 20-second one acts as a recall.

It's true that 15-second commercials are becoming fashionable in the United States. We have had them for a long time because of budgetary constraints. Our market being smaller, longer commercials are incredibly expensive. Don't forget however that it does not cost less to shoot a 15-second commercial than one that lasts one minute. The saving is only in the media price.

QUESTION: A number of U.S. agencies have affiliates in France and all over Europe. To what extent do you think their commercials differ from yours?

MARCUS: It depends more on the client than on the agency. The Ford commercial I have shown, for instance, was an example of an American agency producing a French style film for an American advertiser. Detergent companies, however, are totally reluctant to run that sort of advertising. Maybe they're right, I don't know. Some advertisers have a culture that doesn't allow for the French style of creativity and use as standard procedure a type of research that would kill it. It's more a problem of firm culture than of nationality.

QUESTION: You have said that French advertising is based on long-term goals—creating an impression and an image—while it seems that American advertising is oriented to the short term. Is there a comparative study that shows that long-term advertising works?

MARCUS: You see, advertising is not an art; it is a tool of marketing. Whatever the advertising you run, you stop it if it doesn't sell.

There are not two kinds of advertising. There might be two styles, but the ultimate goal is the same, and you find that it works or maybe doesn't work. If the Maggi films had not worked, we would have stopped them after six months. The Heineken films that you have seen today have helped the brand to reach first place in its market segment in France after five years.

Tests could make you make the wrong decision, but you cannot argue with sales figures. Clients want results and they're right; that's why they advertise.

QUESTION: How would you compare the cost of making a commercial in the United States to making one in France? For example, the rights for music, model costs, and so on.

MARCUS: I think that if the quality is comparable, so are the costs. We have the same problems with the rights for music and the cost of models. This is not surprising because the world of models and the world of music are both very international.

QUESTION: With the privatization of French TV, advertisements will break in shows and films in France as they do in America. How do you think this is going to affect your commercials?

MARCUS: It won't change the ways we develop commercials. It might change the attitude of the public but, for the moment, only the private channels have introduced commercial breaks in films. If people don't like it, they can watch the public channels on which advertising is concentrated before and after the main shows.

QUESTION You have been working with your clients for over twenty years. I was wondering if it was totally unthinkable in the United States to have a client for so long?

MARCUS: Some of the major American firms have not changed agencies for more than twenty years. About ten years ago, the president of General Foods declared: ''I never change agencies because when something goes wrong I get more from my present agency than I would from a new one.'' And I completely share that point of view. If you have problems, and the agency is no good any more, then you must change. But as long as you get good service and have a good professional relationship, you shouldn't change. It's true that we've been working with Nestlé since 1952, with Shell since 1956, with Renault since 1961, and with DIM since 1964. And occasionally we get some new clients, too.

QUESTION: What uses are made in the advertising and public relations business of film or audiovisual presentations outside of television broadcast and cinema? Such possibilities as trade shows where the audience may be small, industrial shows, etc.

MARCUS: The Americans are much better than we are at that sort of presentation.

QUESTION: What kind of state control do you have over what you've been doing?

MARCUS: There is state control only on national television for channels 2 and 3, which belong to the state. Otherwise, there is no control at all.

QUESTION: Do you have any idea what the advertising budget is in French companies as compared to American companies?

MARCUS: They are perfectly comparable for those who have succeeded. For approximately the last fifteen years, L'Oréal has been spending proportionately as much as Revlon, and BSN (Kronenbourg, Danone, Evian, etc.) as much as General Foods. Our problem, an economic one, is that we do not have enough advertising from smaller companies; small business and store advertising is not as developed in France as it is in the United States.

EDITORS' REMARKS

As Jean Boissonnat has shown, the tastes of the French public have changed. As a result, so have the ways business presents itself to the French public. Business news is widely available, and stock market fluctuations make front page news even in the left-wing press. Advertising, which the French once considered to be the worst cultural manifestation of capitalism, is today almost a publicly accepted art form. In many ways it is far more sophisticated than our own. Anglo-Saxon visitors to France are often shocked by revealing French billboards and television advertisements, even for political candidates.

Luxury goods have long been the symbol of French culture at home and abroad. We associate these industries with an older, more traditional France, divided by class distinctions, where luxury was reserved for society's elite.

Have the changes we have described in the previous chapters affected this industry for which the French have so long been famous? Is there a contradiction between luxury goods and a mass market?

The three F's—fashion, fragrance, and food—are also successful modern industries. They are important to the French balance of trade; a large part of advertising spending goes for luxury products. In his presentation, André Doucet describes the impact of mass advertising on the luxury goods industry. Advertising has opened up broad new global markets, but this popularization of luxury goods has created a challenge for managers in the industry. On the one hand, luxury goods are now sought-after popular products; Hermès bags and Dior perfumes now reach consumers the world over. But, on the other hand, this popularity implies a "vulgarization" of luxury products, a dilution of their image as sought-after elite goods.

4

Marketing Luxury Goods

André Doucet

What follows derives from my experience with S. T. Dupont, where I served as president, and my membership in the Colbert Committee, as association of seventy houses that represent the great names of the French luxury business: Baccarat, Chaumet, Chanel, Dior, S. T. Dupont, Christofle; Möet et Chandon, Martell; the George V hotel, the Plaza Athénée; and decorators like Didier Aaron and Canovas, to list only a few.

The luxury industry has traditionally been a major French activity and one of the principal exporters in France. In 1985, for example, houses of the Colbert Committee had sales of FF 18 billion, of which 71 percent came from exports; the Committee ranked fifteenth among all French exporters. Together, the houses employ 24,000 people, who contribute fifty times more to exports than the average French employee. The breakdown of exports follows: 21 percent to Europe; 21 percent to North America; 20 percent to Asia and the Pacific; 9 percent to the Middle East and the rest of the world. This export business, while reasonably distributed, would be more homogeneous and even greater if trade barriers against luxury products did not exist in all Latin American markets.

LUXURY PRODUCTS

Before considering the evolution of the luxury market, we should understand what "luxury" means and what constitutes a luxury product. For the houses of the Colbert Committee, *le luxe* is the part of a dream of desire that lets one forget the practical and enjoy the frivolous; using something for pleasure. Most luxury products were born of a creator who was able to superimpose his or her personal view on an object—a piece of luggage, a dress, a saddle, an item in silver: Vuitton, Chanel, Hermès, Christofle, for example. These names survived the transitory objects that made both the objects and the creators famous. The origin of these brand names involved two factors: fashion and artistic craftsmanship.

Coco Chanel once said, "Fashion is what is going out of fashion." Great couturiers like Chanel, Lanvin, or Saint Laurent, in fact, sign their names to products that are naturally transitory, accessories that evolve with fashion and follow the taste of the times. This "fashion" origin determines, to a certain degree, the nature of the products that these names can sustain. On the other hand, brands born from a craftsman like Christofle, Hermès, or S. T. Dupont support objects that involve a specific technical skill, savoir-faire, know-how, or mastery. Over the years there has been confusion in these types.

A luxury object is perceived on two levels. A beautiful object can be seen as a status symbol, an indication of belonging to a particular social group; the owner is identified with a system of cultural references. At the same time, there is the perception of an object belonging to a category, but this perception is more esthetic than technical: Technical reliability is implicit, and quality is expected to follow naturally. (Unhappily, as will be later shown, not all luxury brands currently justify these assumptions.)

Superimposed on the intrinsic value of a luxury product is an immaterial value: the brand's image. This value changes with the product's success and the brand name's prestige. Ultimately, luxury products are valued based on the price people pay for them, which is directly a function of the reputation and fame of the brand name.

What has been common to all luxury brands, however, is the fact that they were international and that there was limited diffusion: Only some people could own them, and that fact was widely recognized. This has been the principal dimension of luxury products.

Thus, a luxury brand can originate with a unique product, but a true luxury name transcends the product. Chanel does not simply convey the idea of clothing but of elegance; Baccarat does not imply only crystal but a certain lifestyle.

THE LUXURY MARKET

The luxury market is unlimited because it is the domain of the superfluous. There are limits to needs but not to desires. "Need" is only a distant pretext to creating a product, and the only constraint on its multiplication is that of the creator's imagination and the audience's acceptance. So, a luxury product's success—and its market—are unpredictable. Success is the result of a fortuitous meeting of a sociological trend and an object that best expresses it at a given time. The product "signs" an era at such a point that it remains associated with the era in the collective memory. The "New Look" of Dior, the furniture of Leleu, Lalique flasks, Louis Cartier's jewelry—these have "marked" their times.

Another example is the Mont Blanc pen. There is great nostalgia associated with this product's current success. The pen recalls an era, the 1930s, during which, it is presumed, one freely expressed one's individuality with a unique style of handwriting.

The luxury market is also affected by geography. There is, for example, a greater audience for personal luxury objects in the Mediterranean countries, in South America, the Near East, in Southeast Asia because in these countries no one feels guilty about luxury. People wear their social status—jewelry, fine clothing—these are signs of social recognition. Luxury must be shown! By contrast, in Anglo-Saxon countries with their Puritan traditions, luxury is not shown. Luxury needs to be earned, justified: The beautiful house is for the family, the swimming pool for the children, an elegant car for going to work. Luxury is a gift from God and cannot be frivolous; exhibiting it without justification would be obscene.

A final characteristic of the luxury market is the risk that weighs down on the future of a successful product: popularization. The public creates a double bind for luxury products: They must be everlasting and exclusive, precisely what success will help destroy. Because luxury is elitist, luxury products must be continually renewed without making their predecessors unfashionable; that is, to ensure change within continuity. Only fidelity to a secure, well-established style enables a company to do this.

Another risk of popularization is more serious: counterfeiting. As soon as a product becomes internationally renowned, despite all precautions taken, it is prey to counterfeiting. Fakes by the thousands invade the market. Such parasiting not only cuts revenues, worse, it damages distribution networks and destroys the brand's image—to the point of ruining the best known.

EVOLUTION OF THE LUXURY MARKET

During the 1970s, a luxury brand's fame was based—as it has been for decades—on craftsmanship, a particular expertise that was expressed in prestigious objects. The public recognized the brand as leading in the creation and manufacturing of a certain type of object: a saddle for Hermès, crystal for Baccarat, for example. Reputations were built slowly, and it was not necessary to renew products constantly to maintain those reputations.

The luxury objects themselves were totally identified with the brands: One said "a Dupont," "a Rolex," "a Hermès bag." The objects were simultaneously exclusive, durable, with proven quality and reliability. The product in itself was the most perfect and authentic expression of the brand name; the brand was restricted to the "signature" of the product and constituted, by extension, its guarantee.

All this had consequences in the market: The market was stable and was sliced in product categories from which "reference objects" began to emerge. Some brands in each category, through their savoir-faire, talent and reputation, began to constitute a sort of envied and admired aristocracy. And although most of the major luxury brands used international advertising, its cost in relation to the cost of the product remained a relatively modest 15–20 percent.

The market of the 1970s then can be divided into two categories. First there is the luxury market linking fashion to its accessories: bags, belts, shoes, costume jewelry, and of course, perfumes, which are a natural extension of the great couture houses. Overall, these luxury products were generally high priced, had a brief life, and were frequently purchased. The second category is the market of luxury investments consisting of objects from craftsmen: watches, jewelry, cigarette lighters, and luggage, for example. Each luxury brand, depending on its type, was clearly positioned in one of the two categories: Each brand name corresponded to a particular type of product and no other.

At the end of the 1970s and the beginning of the 1980s, there was a radical change in the luxury market that influenced all brands—French or not: a universalization of the luxury market and an acceleration of products being renewed. This change occurred:

• because the lifestyles of a privileged class, which transcends national borders and constitutes the principal clientele for luxury products, became globalized;

• because what was "fashionable" was diffused with supersonic speed—by global media and through international travel, so that fashion was imitated by larger and larger groups of people;

• because of international distribution networks—from department stores to airport boutiques—that relay a brand's "message" in the same form worldwide;

• because the "media-ization" of what is in fashion accelerates its globalization.

In order to communicate easily with this dispersed clientele from different cultures that traveled as a matter of course, luxury companies sought to give themselves an image as synthetic and standardized as possible. The brand name became a kind of symbol, a global publicity concept that expressed at the same time a product, a craft, a country of origin, a history, a tradition, an original style, and an esthetic atmosphere.

Adopting the formula of Valéry that "what is simple is false but what is complicated is useless," most luxury houses, rather than adjust their messages to different markets, sought to make their brands a kind of universal passport. Hence, the product has progressively lost ground to the brand.

This disconnecting of the brand and its products, the preeminence of the brand over the product, almost substituting the brand for the product to the point that it is not the product that must be sold but the brand; this has encouraged most luxury houses to enter the path of despecialization. With increasing frequency, attempts to maximize a brand's image on the luxury market have resulted in luxury investment products that go beyond traditional categories. For example, Dunhill, a leader in luxury accessories for smokers, has had a true reconversion, transferring much of its efforts into textiles, a sector that now represents 55 percent of its sales. Cartier, in the same way, has successfully launched a perfume that now represents nearly 8 percent of its revenues. Each company strove to grab its share of the luxury market that is not only permeable but profitable. The products have strong value added and are repurchased frequently.

Likewise, many couturiers have entered the domain of luxury investment products. Dior, Céline, Saint Laurent, and Cardin, among others, have attached their names to a variety of objects heretofore in the investment product areas: lighters, watches, luggage, dishes, linen—who knows what else. We have even seen luxury brand names on consumer products: Dunhill whiskey, Cardin jelly!

This despecialization of brand names has made the distinction between luxury investment products and luxury products connected to fashion increasingly blurred; at the same time a tremendous qualitative revolution has occurred on the luxury market. The product—the object of everyone's attention—has been superseded by the brand, the logo, the initials.

A reputation earned as a result of craftsmanship, competence, and quality has been replaced by a renown based too often on a series of processes completely alien to the product. For example, "sponsoring" has superimposed on the product the image of the intended user: sports figures, members of the jet set, movie stars. A variable, "brand name show biz," has been put in place by middlemen.

Furthermore, too many luxury names have lost control of the development of their product lines. Offering under a brand umbrella a variety of products, numerous companies have strayed onto perilous paths, without guarantees from subcontractors or with excessive licensing. Ignorant of the technologies of products sold under their name, not controlling after-sale servicing, they have relinquished one of their principal prerogatives: the assurance of quality. To finance heavier and heavier advertising expenses as well as to make money more easily, these companies have let slip the true attribute of luxury and the source of its legitimacy: quality.

What these products have lost in intrinsic value has been compensated for by "brand-name theater" (*marque-spectacle*): "staging" products, ostentatious packaging, opening of boutiques in prestige locations with much fanfare, thundering public relations efforts devoted to regilding an image.

Hence, appearance, guaranteed by a logo or initials, is too often substituted for content: The image is substituted for the product; what is essential has become an accessory. At the extreme, the luxury product has become something for which one has enthusiasm, then purchases, and throws away. The quality, reliability, and durability of the product matters little, as long as it correctly expresses the fashion of the moment, a fashion that the brand name assures and its advertising supports. It no longer matters if the life of the object, like the life of the fashion it represents, is ephemeral. We have entered the age of throwaway luxury.

This situation is the result of a great confusion between the luxury product— a subtle combination of innovation, style, intrinsic quality, post-sale services— and the "in" product, whose success is entirely based on fashion and the magic of communication. (The proportion of advertising and public relations in the selling price continues to mount, to the point of exceeding the intrinsic cost of the product.)

CONCLUSION

The media explosion in the luxury market and its resulting excesses have prompted most French luxury houses to search their souls and redefine the values upon which they should base their development strategy. Some bet on ephemeral fashion accessories supported by an intense advertising barrage, and base their strategy on always being one step ahead of the game. This can work, although there have been brand names that have died from overdose. What kills luxury brands, frequently, is not old age but excess! Others opt for the long term, and confine themselves to authentic luxury objects of style, endurance, and with that uncompromising quality that constitutes the expensive privilege of truly great luxury names.

So, facing these alternatives, companies must clearly position themselves and adjust their commercial philosophies accordingly.

What can we say about the current customers of luxury products?

- that the well-informed customer to whom these products are addressed, having been influenced by the media, is in the process of regaining his independent judgment;
- that this customer, having been abused by certain "dream merchants," having succumbed to the show biz of certain brands, is now in search of authenticity—and he knows, having been taught by sad experience, how to distinguish the true luxury from the false;
- that in this era of great instability there is a genuine consumer demand for products that are reassuring in their quality and durability;
- finally, pushing the analysis to the limit, we discover that quality is in itself a true value of civilization. Nothing can endure if it is not built with lasting quality.

Based on this analysis, most of the houses of the Colbert Committee have established an ethical code as rigorous and stringent as the era is lax. They recognize:

- that the great luxury brands have the prerogative of educating the public, as they always have, in beauty and taste, through the elegance and excellence of their products;
- that they have the duty but also the privilege of putting their stamp on an era through objects whose style transcends fashion of the moment. These houses are now more attentive than ever that their development takes place in accordance with some cardinal virtues: innovation, style, fair pricing, quality, obsession with perfection, pre- and post-sale service, and the product's surroundings.

This philosophy of rediscovered luxury around which the great French names are rallying has its own logic based on four objectives. First of all, to ensure a lasting style integral to a brand's identity requires in-house designers and a styling group that is a vigilant guardian of the image. Second, to ensure quality, which requires in-house manufacturing or strict control over subcontractors. The third objective, craftsmanship, requires protecting, training, and renewing those crafts- men who have raised their skills to incomparable levels and the reputation of the houses that employ them to the highest level. These skills are transmitted from generation to generation, and this artisanal tradition must be preserved or the source of the exclusive luxury object will dry up. Finally, it is important to closely control the distribution of luxury products. This is what prompted many houses in recent years to open their own boutiques in major cities worldwide. Stores with identical architecture, displaying products in a similar manner, pric- ing them similarly accomplish the following:

- communicating to the public an image that is as strong and standardized as possible;
- protecting the product, via strict distribution, against practices like dumping and un- controlled competition, which would adversely affect the brand image;
- surrounding the product with pre- and post-sale service, which is inseparable from a luxury product. Pre-sale service is information, advice, choice; post-sale service means following up throughout the product's life;
- and, because nothing can be done without money, gaining sufficient manufacturing and distribution margins to finance international advertising. For example, Louis Vuitton, which in 1980 had only one boutique in the United States and whose distribution was fairly fragmented, has subsequently grown, so that in 1986 there were twenty-five boutiques, accounting for most of its sales.

Houses of the Colbert Committee are dedicated to prosecuting counterfeiters rigorously, for they discredit the product and degrade the brand image and its reputation, confusing the buyer's perception.

Thus, the great luxury brands strive, through the products they promote, the stores they open, the advertising and public relations they diffuse, to build into a brand name an emotional content, because luxury is passion before reason. They also strive to build in a cultural esthetic, directly linked to a national tradition. A brand name, like an individual, needs roots; it needs to be from somewhere.

This then is how the great French luxury houses are positioning themselves. They adapt to the market without giving into it; they distance themselves from the present, which is the true attribute of aristocracy. They do not deviate from the values upon which luxury is based. The houses of the Colbert Committee continue their development knowing that prestige, international renown, are earned day after day, product after product, customer after customer. They also recognize that innovation, quality, and service are inseparable and are the only guarantee of real success.

PART IV

Continuity and Change in the Workplace

I

Trade Unions

Yves-Frédéric Livian

We are witnessing one of the most original periods in the area of industrial relations in France. The country's particular situation is not easy for a foreign observer to understand and is even more difficult to grasp. Yet, the evolution that France experiences today in this field merits attention. Some journalists and politicians are speaking about the "modernization of labor-management relations" in the same way as we have been speaking about industrial modernization for the past few years. In fact, we are referring here to a true silent transformation.

I shall begin this analysis of the present situation with a brief overview of the evolution of France's political and legal environment. More precisely, we will look at the evolution of various stakeholders or interests. The system lives through them and it is at this level that important changes are appearing.

THE EVOLUTION OF THE POLITICAL AND LEGAL ENVIRONMENT

It is impossible to separate the evolution of industrial relations in France from this country's recent political history because each majority party (the Socialist majority from 1981 to 1986 and then the Right-wing majority since 1986) has had a different conception of industrial relations.

The Socialist government, in 1982, originated an important legal change: One-third of the Labor Code was modified that year. The project was known by the name *Loi Auroux* (the name of the minister of labor at that time). Its objective was to strengthen the unions' presence within companies, to develop direct negotiations between business and labor on social issues, and to better protect employee representatives elected by their peers to serve on work councils or to act as intermediaries between labor and management. This basic concept was close to "industrial democracy" so often referred to in the 1960s in Scandinavian countries.

The government elected in March 1986 preferred to defend a liberal policy (in the French sense of the term) and tried to modify legislation in terms of what is considered best for French industry: more flexibility, fewer rules and regulations, less state intervention.

However, contrary to what some of its supporters suggest, the new policy does not basically modify the legislation. Once again, we see a sociological law, perhaps peculiar to France, in action: In the area of labor-management relations it is difficult to take a step backwards and return to previous policies. Even those laws that were severely criticized by employers in 1982 were not eliminated in 1986.

Some legislation was relaxed. For example, certain state interventions were eliminated, the most important decision being to no longer require administrative authorization for layoffs due to downturns in business. Nevertheless, the main trend of the legal process has not been reversed, most likely because it corresponds to a profound change taking place in thinking. This evolution may be summarized in three essential parts:

1. Enhancing the Power of Elected Personnel Representatives in the *Comité d'entreprise* or Work Councils

The basic structure for mutual discussion and information exchange between employers and wage earners' representatives in French companies is the *comité d'entreprise* (C.E.). It was created in 1945 and is composed of employees elected by a company's personnel, generally from union lists. Its goal, in companies with more than fifty employees, is "to assure a collective voice for employees" and "to influence decisions that directly concern employees."

The final decision always remains solely with the boss, who presides over the *comité d'entreprise*, or board of directors. There is no policy of mutual decision making or codetermination. However, the law and its implementation have defined more widespread areas where management has certain obligations to the committee. These areas are essentially in the area of informing and consulting with employees.

First of all, information to be shared includes:

• information about economic, commercial, and financial management of the company. For example, once a year, a discussion based on the company's annual report should take place. The C.E. can even summon auditors in order to have explanations about the financial status of the company;

• information on employment problems and working conditions;

• information concerning new technologies;

• information on health or safety problems;

• even more important, the committee must be informed and consulted on working hours, employment, training, and continuing education.

Finally, the committee can directly assume responsibility for or control the management of cultural or social activities beneficial to employees and their families. These are called *social functions*, and include leisure and sports activities, company restaurants, summer camps for children, and the like.

The basic functions of the C.E. and discussions with management have existed for years, but the recent trend has been to reinforce the power of the committee. For example, in companies with more than 1,000 employees, an economic committee is responsible for studying in detail economic documents passed on by management. In large companies having several subsidiaries, a company committee is required not only in each subsidiary, but at the group level. This did not exist before.

In practice, of course, the situation is very different from one company to the other. Elected employee representatives are more or less interested in one category of information and tend to be more rigorous in that area. This varies depending on the company's economic situation. However, if these representatives are elected from the most influential unions within the company, this form of obligatory discussion and exchange will evolve towards a negotiation process.

In general, these committees, strengthened by legislation, constitute a basic element in the French system of industrial relations.

2. The Strengthening of Unions' Role in Companies

The role given to unions, by law, has not ceased growing over the years. (This does not imply that the real role of unions or their power has increased, as shall be discussed below.) This role was recognized for the first time in 1968. The specific goals of several measures, taken in 1982, were to help in the development and protection of employee representatives and, more precisely, union delegates.

First of all, it became possible for unions to establish a presence in every firm, even the smallest; previously this could occur only in firms with more than fifty employees. In France, as opposed to the United States, a union can exist in a company without having to prove that it represents a majority of employees. It is enough for a few employees to take the initiative of officially informing management of the union's existence.

Next, once a year, in every company where there is a union, management must negotiate salaries and the duration and organization of work with the unions in the company at that time. This is similar to a system in Québec. Of course, there is no obligation to conclude a contract. One cannot force the two parties to agree. However, negotiations must be real and seriously undertaken.

Finally, other rights have been agreed to. These include allowing unions to use company facilities for meetings, making it more difficult to lay off elected employee delegates, and allowing unions to invite well-known union activists from outside the company to participate in meetings inside the company.

3. Increasing Employees' Right to Free Expression in the Workplace

One of the most innovative points in the 1982 laws was the formulation of labor's right to free expression within the workplace, which refers to their right to express themselves on how work is organized and working conditions. This was, in many firms, really a "new" freedom, although some companies had already set up various types of meetings to exchange ideas and opinions or discussion groups to reinforce the rising tide of greater communication. In addition, free expression is a right that may be exercised outside of union proceedings. The law refers to direct free speech, without any intermediaries, which appears contradictory to the hope of strengthening unions just mentioned. This explains why almost all the unions that were in fact generally in agreement with the "Auroux Laws" were firmly against this particular point. They felt it was too directly inspired by management's wishes and threatened the union's role as intermediary between business and labor.

The law was never implemented as fully as its supporters had hoped. It has at times been invoked by management, which tried to use it when faced with rather unenthusiastic unions. Also this right to "direct expression" competed with another important development, quality circles. Many managers gave first priority to this latter form of free expression. In spite of very evident differences both in their original inspiration and practical application, these forms of expressing opinions and ideas add another cornerstone to a process that appears irreversible and that corresponds to the aspirations of many workers, who wish to be able to express themselves on concrete elements of their working life, using intermediaries as little as possible.

THE EVOLUTION OF BUSINESS AND LABOR RELATIONS

The Unions in a Time of Crisis

One of the paradoxes of the French situation is that just when the left-wing party came to power, with very active support from the unions, these unions were gradually weakening in number and influence. This was much the same phenomenon found in other industrial countries.

If we try to summarize the strengths and weaknesses of French unions, the following points are pertinent.

Union organizations are influential in many areas; it has been traditional to reserve seats for union delegates in a number of regional commissions, boards of directors, labor-management benefit organizations, and university boards. Unions also play a major management role in various social security commissions. In addition, they participate in committees that have decision-making power in the management of civil service personnel. Unions are a sort of institution, an official part of French society, and until very recently, they had a great deal of credibility in the public's eyes. Certain survey polls revealed that a majority of French recognize the role unions should play on a national level, yet many of those same people were not necessarily union members.

Finally, within the workplace the number of company unions has risen since 1968, when they were officially recognized. In 1970, 27.5 percent of French companies with more than fifty employees had a union local; by 1981, this reached 60 percent.

But there are signs that unions are weakening. Membership levels, traditionally between 23–24 percent, have fallen today to close to 15 percent, one of the lowest levels of any industrialized country. Of course, this does not prevent the various unions from reaching impressive scores in delegate elections. In France, one may vote in an election for the works council (*comité d'entreprise*), selecting one's candidates, for example, from a union list without being a member of that union. However, the members' dues represent a financial resource, and these people are the ones who will support union actions, be present at meetings, read the press, and hand out leaflets.

In France, being a union member is never an obligation and never gives any additional material advantages. The closed shop does not exist. For this reason, belonging to a union is a sort of militant act, which brings no specific advantages. It may in fact be a disadvantage, and create serious problems with company management. Thus, the number of members is an indication of how dynamic a union may be and the kind of rank-and-file support it will receive to attain its objectives. Unionism with few members is inevitably weak unionism, especially if it has also been institutionalized on a national level. The risk is that the unions will become just like any other bureaucracy and receive less and less support from those at the base of the organization.

The major union themes have sounded conservative chords in the past few years, especially in comparison with the practices of some of the most progressive companies. The result, in certain situations, has been that the majority of the employees have agreed with management on particular subjects while the union has been against them. This was the case with flexible working hours; unions were strongly opposed to this proposal at the beginning. This was also the case with employee stock distribution and the use of temporary workers. In each situation unions refused measures that the majority of the employees had accepted, thereby not being the true mouthpiece for all of the demands of labor. Significantly, a recent opinion poll revealed that 60 percent of all employees felt that unions did not really represent their desires. In addition, the number of strike days in France has declined regularly over the last ten years. The rare serious conflicts have been in the public sector, such as the railways strike at the end of 1986, or in companies where the initiative came from the rank and file rather than from union leadership.

Finally, the media play an important role in France, as elsewhere. Unions do not use the media to their fullest possibilities or to their benefit; currently, there are union leaders who in the opinion polls are ranked very low in popularity. This, of course does not help to improve the union movement's image.

A recent event proves this loss of union influence. In the last national elections for the labor courts (Prud'hommes), a conciliation board of employers and workers that settles industrial disputes (made up of delegates, often from union lists, elected by the wage earners and representatives of the employers), the unions, no matter which political tendency, were unable to rally labor. The abstention level, which had already risen from 36.8 percent in 1979 to 41.39 percent in 1982, rose to 54 percent in 1987.

But beyond such evidence, one can analyze the union's position in reference to various sectors of labor in France.

First are the transient employees, those excluded from social benefits such as the unemployed or those who work odd jobs. These people do not expect anything from unions. Demands are difficult to formulate for such a group, made up primarily of younger people, who are known not to be interested in unionism. (An opinion poll completed a few years ago revealed that 45 percent of those between the ages of eighteen and twenty-four did not see themselves as part of any of the five principal unions.)

Next are those employees who work for the numerous companies now being restructured and where employment problems are at the forefront. It is known that employment problems, especially at a time of serious crisis for a firm, prove not to be a favorable moment for efficient union action. At best, unions can only watch over the distribution of social benefits promised to those employees affected by the changes. In these situations, unions do not find fertile ground for organizing. Those who remain are only interested in saving their own jobs.

On the contrary, do unions find a favorable atmosphere in companies that are expanding? Much less than one might think, primarily because these are often small or medium-sized companies where unionism is not strong or where management has innovative social policies.

Finally, there is the public sector, which is relatively well protected from economic difficulties and where unions have always been active. In public agencies, unions are well integrated into everyday affairs and can influence decision making. This is another form of unionism, one that comes very close to defending individual sectoral interests. Those whom the union represents support it unanimously (for example in education, the judiciary, the police). Overall, however, this sector is unique and is not an area where employment could grow.

Thus, in the words of a French union leader, "Unionism is weak where employment is making the most gains."

Less State and Employer Intervention

The Conseil National du Patronat Français (CNPF), the national federation of employers' organizations, very much against the labor-management and economic measures taken by the left-wing government, now sees many of its proposals adopted by the current government. They did not try to overturn the policies inherited from the Left. Instead they have encouraged more flexibility and encouraged decentralized negotiations on the company level. As a result, some employer organizations, which have undergone a crisis in the last few years, have been phased out. Many companies do not hide their desire to preserve a right to independent decision making, even when facing the organizations responsible for representing them. Some decisions that the CNPF approved on a national level have not been respected by individual companies. An internal conflict during the 1987 election of the CNPF very severely undermined the organization. The most recent election to the labor courts, where one slate of management was presented, had a record number of abstentions, 65.93 percent.

Although the state has traditionally been an omnipresent partner in French industrial relations, the present government has tried to reduce its intervention. France's economic situation has necessitated adjustments on a local level and greater flexibility in management.

Even for a liberal government the task is not easy. The state's duty is to respect social legislation, monitor training programs and employment, and watch over the management of social security. The state cannot have a firm economic policy without also influencing companies' human resources choices, particularly in the area of salaries. So the government tried to soften its policy towards employment. It took such steps as making it easier to employ temporary personnel by creating temporary work contracts; it simplified procedures for layoffs. The government also encouraged management and union delegates to work directly together in certain areas. This form of direct negotiation is so foreign to French practice that the government is sometimes obliged to pressure one of the two parties by threatening to intervene if they do not reach an agreement.

What is remarkable, and constitutes a veritable reversal of French attitudes in this area, is the recent awareness of the overregulation of labor relations. Without going as far as burning the Labor Code, as a publication predicted in 1985, the present government and the Parliament are trying to introduce the concept of flexibility. As early as 1982, signed agreements between employers and unions could diverge from the law if it was necessary economically. Previously, a union-employer agreement could only be a supplementary measure to the law, which provided a minimum amount of protection to labor. More and more, the agreements on new regulations could move away from the law if both sides agreed. The social legislation acted as a pivot. This role is beginning to fade as direct and free negotiations develop between the two parties concerned.

Individual Firms in the Forefront

The most important element in the current evolution is negotiations developing on a company level. In 1983, 1,955 company agreements were signed; in 1986 there were 6,600. This trend leads to the disappearance of centralized employer structures that were used to negotiate nationally or across industry. This also adds to the difficulties the unions are experiencing, for their structure is likewise more adapted to centralized negotiating. Traditionally, French unionism has been opposed to individual company unionism. Such a movement is vulnerable to charges of favoritism.

These changes are not recent. The obligation to negotiate mentioned previously also moved in this same direction, even if it has provoked much discussion. However, in particular, French economic circumstances and the need to modernize industry have led to less rigorous regulation and to the avoidance of nationwide general agreements. Unlike the 1970s, industry agreements are not being negotiated, and even those within the same sector are increasingly obsolete. Now negotiations are more often carried out on an individual company level. During a time of economic crisis and great technological change, discussions concerning, for example, the organization of working hours, find their natural place within the company, even on the shop floor.

An evolution from within the union movement also favors the company itself as the essential place for negotiations. The CGT, the union leading the anticapitalist fight, is constantly losing ground, even though it remains the largest French union. During the last ten years, unofficial figures indicate that this union lost at least half of its membership. In the board of directors elections for social security, the CGT got 28.25 percent of the vote in 1986, as opposed to 60 percent in 1983.

The only union to progress is FO (Force Ouvrière), which represents moderates and leans toward negotiations. As for the socialist CFDT, in the last few years it has adopted an attitude open to dialogue on economic issues with employers. This union has even gone far in supporting local wage concessions; it has also negotiated other measures destined to save jobs in companies that are threatened financially. A number of unions agreed to give up cost-of-living adjustments, an important issue for the last ten years. Some agreements have established wage funds, meaning that wage earners agree to freeze a part of their salary and lend this sum to the company to help overcome financial difficulties. There was much discussion about an agreement signed in a large glass company, BSN. Management accepted a considerable reduction in working time (to around thirty-three hours per week) for line workers. In exchange, workers agreed to a 7 percent increase in productivity. For the first time, all unions, even the CGT, signed an agreement whereby the employees were asked to give up rights. The media largely exploited this event, but it is true that it marked a turning point in the evolution of the French system.

One last current development converges in the same direction: the distribution of stock to employees. Several million wage earners bought shares in their companies in 1986 and 1987 during the move toward privatization. This reveals how feelings have changed towards companies, and such an evolution cannot be ignored.

One must be careful not to conclude that industrial relations in France are beginning to resemble those in the United States, although this would not displease certain French managers. Systematic negotiations based on mutual commitment do not exist in France. The unions are weaker and have a completely different conception of their role. Although much closer, the West German system differs from that of the French in the power and capacity of the two partners to agree. Also, codetermination, which also exists in Germany, is incompatible with French managers' understanding of their authority and how French unions see their mission.

Nevertheless, it is certain that the period of economic change France has just experienced has altered the course of industrial relations. It is also interesting to note that political changes have not modified this evolution. Most observers agree that a true modernization of industrial relations is actually taking place, even though they do not state this point of view too openly; social consensus in France is still considered a bit suspect.

French Women in Business

Beatrice Dautresme
Lydie Bonnet

EDITORS' REMARKS

When the topic "The Role of Women in French Business" (the original title of the session) was proposed for the Harvard colloquium on French Business in 1987, a number of young French women reacted by replying that there is "no difference in the role of women in France or in the United States; it's the same all over." The session was nonetheless included in the conference program, because our purpose was neither to prove nor disprove the uniqueness of the French woman's role in business, but rather to describe what that role is. The session began with some general information on women in the French work force and results of a survey of attitudes toward work. We have expanded these introductory comments here to provide a context for two of the personal accounts of work experiences presented by French businesswomen at the Harvard colloquium. Finally, we have included audience remarks that shed additional light on the role of women in business in France.

MODERATOR: Although many people, especially women, tend to view the role of women in business as determined entirely by the business environment, in fact, the role of women in business, French or otherwise, is determined by both personal and external factors. The position a woman holds is affected by her level of education, her need to earn money, and her degree of ambition. Regardless of the structure of the business organization, women will attain positions of importance only if they are adequately prepared educationally, are willing to accept responsibility, and have the drive to succeed.

In the United States and France, and probably in other countries as well, the role that women play in business is a result of economic, environmental, and social factors. The receptivity of business to women managers and executives varies from sector to sector, and depends also on the number of employees. In addition, geography influences a woman's chance to get ahead, with misogyny inversely proportional to population; in other words, women in business seem to be more accepted in the larger cities.

Although many people have the impression that French women traditionally do not work outside the home, this is not true. A significant number of French women have always been present in the work force, the percentage varying from a high of 52 percent in 1921 to a low of 36 percent in the 1960s. At present, 45 percent of French women over the age of fifteen hold jobs in agriculture, industry, and business, in the public and private sectors.[1] There are 10.5 million women working in France, a percentage higher than in Great Britain or West Germany and equal to that in the United States.[2]

While the number of French women working has varied but not changed significantly since the beginning of the century, women are no longer doing the same type of work, having deserted the farms for offices. In 1901, 43.6 percent of the women working were in agriculture, while in 1983 that percentage dropped to 7.5 percent. At the same time the proportion of women in services, including education, medicine, law, and the civil service, has soared to 72.5 percent. In fact, 43 percent of the women in France are concentrated in five job categories, four in the service sector: semiskilled work, secretarial services, general office work, sales, and cleaning services.[3] This situation is perpetuated because young women continue to choose the same type of work their mothers did, avoiding technical professions for a variety of reasons. The service sector is a safe bet, a hospitable area in which, until recently, women were assured jobs since it was expanding rapidly. On the other hand, women have never entered industry in massive numbers, 20 percent of women working in manufacturing in 1983 and never more than 30 percent since 1906.

In spite of the fact that almost half of all women over the age of fifteen work, there are always fewer women than men working, at lower echelons and for lower salaries. The difference in numbers reflects social attitudes and practices. One interpretation is that more than 90 percent of men between the ages of nineteen and fifty are employed, while the percentage varies from 70 percent to 50 percent for women, because work is perceived as an obligation for men but as a choice for women. However, one can explain this discrepancy by empirically observed situations as well as by attitude. For example, there are fewer women than men under the age of twenty-five working, because young women in France tend to continue their education longer than do young men. Fewer women over fifty-five work, because in France that is the age at which women can retire. The percentage of women over twenty-five in the work force also depends on the number of children they have; 60 percent of mothers work, but only 40 percent of those with three children or more work. In general, the more education a woman has, the more likely she is to work; in France, 39 percent of women without a high school diploma work, as compared to 74 percent of those who have a college degree.[4]

The lower salaries women receive (in spite of a series of laws guaranteeing equal pay for equal work regardless of sex) and their concentration at lower levels can be attributed to a variety of factors. Although young women continue their education longer than men, they are often less qualified for jobs requiring technical skills. At the same time, they profit less from the on-the-job training that employers by law must offer their employees, either because their family responsibilities prevent them from taking advantage of courses that meet at night or in a distant location, or because their employers find them more valuable in their low-skilled jobs. Women often work in low-paying sectors in France, such as textiles or publishing, or in small businesses that pay lower wages and provide fewer social benefits than larger companies. On the factory floor, women are excluded from higher-paying jobs, either because the law forbids them from working at night (a law recently changed) or because they are doing work that requires manual dexterity but not physical force, the latter being remunerated at a higher rate than the former. In addition, women with children have less seniority because of their maternity leaves.

French women have, however, made great strides in obtaining managerial and executive positions in the last twenty years due to favorable legislation and increased educational opportunities. A series of laws has established the principle of equal pay for equal work (1972), made sex discrimination illegal in hiring (1975), and codified professional equality, making sex discrimination illegal in any work situation (1983). Previously all-male graduate schools—Polytechnique and HEC, for example—whose diplomas are a ticket to success in French business, have been opened to women since the early 1970s. Polytechnique is now 8 percent female, and more than 40 percent of HEC students are women. In addition, in both the civil service, the employer of almost half of French working women,[5] and banking, internal exams allow professional advancement to all regardless of sex.

As a result, there are more and more women executives in France, but there is great contrast between impressions, opinions, and statistics regarding their situation. First, there is the problem of what an executive is. The French word *cadre* has been used to designate those with managerial status, originally referring to top management, or executives, but has gradually been broadened to include nearly anyone with supervisory responsibility. Statistical analyses of the work force in France still use the word *cadre*, not always separating this catchall category into its significant subgroups. Therefore, while it is possible to point to women's growing importance in French business by citing the fact that they represented only 30 percent of cadres in the early 1960s but 40 percent in 1984, at the same time it is necessary to point out that only 25 percent of upper-level executives, 6 percent of engineers, and 2.5 percent of the highest level of civil servants are women. In addition, this increase in numbers is attributed more to improvements in education than to a change in mentality. For example, in a recent survey, although gender was not a consideration in hiring practices for 60 percent of the companies questioned, 20 percent of the firms had only one woman manager, or none at all. This discrepancy is a result of a lack of change in the stereotypical image of women that predominates. Those who do not hire women claim that they are inflexible with regard to time schedules, but 80 percent of those who hire women find that they accept irregular schedules and business travel, and have no greater a rate of absenteeism than men. More important and damaging are the notions about what women can and cannot do. In the study already mentioned, those who don't hire women think that women are unable to assert themselves in traditional masculine sectors, and that women have interpersonal problems in both sales and personnel functions. Forty-four percent of those who don't hire women and 22 percent of those who do hire women think that the role of men is to decide and that of women to organize, thereby illustrating one of the unwritten policies that keep women from the top positions where decisions are made.[6] In the same way, women factory workers are kept on the assembly line in electronics or small machinery manufacturing plants because they are prized for their manual dexterity and attention to detail, supposedly feminine traits.

The French seem to accept the fact that some sectors are masculine or feminine, and women orient their careers in the context of this limitation. The insurance, rubber, aviation, computer, and construction industries are considered masculine, while public relations is seen as feminine. Within a company, women tend to work in the areas of personnel, communication, finance, and training but are rarely in production or engineering.[7] Even women succumb to the myths or refuse to buck the realities that restrict women to certain sectors and jobs. For example, a woman director of marketing for a lock manufacturer said she hired only male sales representatives because construction is a male-dominated industry.[8]

The situation has changed to the extent that a recent article claims that women "have conquered all the professional citadels previously occupied by men."[9] However, women's salaries are still lower, by 35 percent in 1984.[10] In addition, both men and women demonstrate resistance to women as bosses or in positions of power or control. More than 60 percent of women questioned said that a woman would never be president of their company, and both men and women overwhelmingly prefer men as bosses.[11]

Most people agree that women who are successful in French business fall into one of three categories: they have graduated from the best schools and therefore have a highly valued diploma; they work in a family business as a result of marriage, inheritance, or widowhood; or they have started their own business. Very few women are CEOs of large companies; in a 1986 study of 5,030 French companies whose sales totaled more than 50 percent of the GDP, only 4.6 percent had a women CEO.[12] When the CEO is a woman, it is often because she has started the company; in 1986, 14,000 women started their own businesses in France.[13] These are often small businesses; women own one-fifth of all small businesses in France, as compared to one-fourth in the United States and one-third in Canada.[14]

In order to understand fully the role of women in French business, we must have more than statistics. For this reason, a recent study tried to ascertain what women themselves thought about their importance, their treatment, and their situation in general as compared to their male counterparts. Twenty women between the ages of twenty and forty-five, with sixteen under the age of thirty-five, responded to a questionnaire. Nearly all lived in the Paris area and were well educated, with only one having the equivalent of a junior college rather than a college diploma, and several having graduate degrees. Only two women were in industry (a small manufacturer and a large computer company); the majority were in services: banking, insurance, publishing, hotel, accounting, and public relations. Most worked in large companies.

Most of these women have a positive attitude toward their insertion in the previously nearly all-male world of business. In general, they think they earn the same salary as a man with the same qualifications, would not have a better job if they were male (although there is less consensus on this point), have the same possibilities for promotion, and have no difficulties in working with male colleagues. In spite of this optimistic outlook, however, nearly all of the women who responded to the questionnaire cited problems inherent in being a woman in French business. First, there was a general feeling that things went well as long as one was on one's guard and was vigilant as to one's rights. As is the sentiment in the United States, the subjects wrote that women have to work harder and be more competent than men to obtain an equivalent position at the same salary. There is also the problem of credibility; it is automatically assumed that a woman is less competent than a man. Anecdotal replies mentioned incidents in which questions were addressed to male co-workers in a meeting even though it was the woman's area of expertise, or of men assuming that any woman who answers the phone is a secretary. Finally, some women found that a woman has difficulty in finding the right balance of flexibility and firmness in work relations, that it is harder for them to assert their authority, and that, as was found in the study already mentioned, men do not want to have a female supervisor.

The most consistent cause mentioned for inequality between men and women in the work place was the factor of family responsibilities for women. One young mother cited the problem of being blocked in a low-level position because she did not want to work full time. One woman stated that she did not have the same possibility for advancement as a man because she was not willing to sacrifice everything for a career. A number of questionnaires stressed the difference in career opportunities depending on sector: human relations and public relations are "feminine" fields in which women have no problem, while there are few women in industry, although one respondent wrote that small companies in the eyeglass industry are dominated by self-made women.

Some women considered their femininity to be an advantage. One woman said that it was easier for a woman to obtain an appointment, that a woman's requests for appointments were refused less easily. Another wrote that a woman can have greater visibility, be noticed more than a male colleague. One bit of advice from an executive in a large company was that women in business should stay feminine without being feminist!

It is interesting to note the difference in attitude between the responses and attitudes of the women under thirty-five and over thirty-five who answered these questionnaires. The younger ones saw few problems in being a woman and, although they agreed that men benefited from an *a priori* acceptance while women have to prove themselves, they envisioned a career free of sexism and similar to that of their male counterparts. On the other hand, the older women cited cases in which they had suffered on the basis of their sex and were quite sure that they would have gone further and faster than men. There are three possible explanations for this difference in attitude. First, the older women have had more experience and have had time to become disillusioned by reality. The second possibility is that the younger women are more educated with highly valued diplomas and therefore have the background and the will to compete on an equal footing with men. The third possibility is that, in fact, times have changed and it is, in reality, easier for a woman to succeed today than it was twenty years ago. In all probability, all three explanations are correct to some extent and, since two out of three indicate progress, we can be optimistic about the future role of women in French business.

DAUTRESME

To assess the position of women in French business in 1987, one must first consider the role they have traditionally played and its evolution. The long-established motto of France is "Liberty, Equality, Fraternity." Equality, a notion conspicuously absent in some crucial areas, has been present in the fundamental area of education. For decades, women in France had free access to higher education on very much an equal footing as men. Prior to the Second World War, women were participating in the fields of medicine, scientific research, and law. It is well established that access to traditional types of education was open to women. The more nebulous area, however, was just how far a woman could progress before she reached the invisible barrier beyond which she could not progress. The advent of the Second World War brought women more actively into the work force in the United States—the era of Rosie the Riveter—and gave them the financial freedom that a weekly paycheck provided. In France, the war's aftermath brought legislation both to encourage birth rates and endow working mothers with a panoply of welfare state–type measures, both in pre- and postnatal care, as well as job security. A structure has been in place in France for decades for some women to enter into professions and others on the less fortunate end of the spectrum to have basic guarantees that are coveted by women in many countries today.

What, then, is the status of the area between these two? Where are the female captains of industry who are visibly absent from our equation? And what has lead to their absence? I remember reading about ten years ago a remark made by Francine Gomez, then chairman of the board of Waterman Pen, stating that in France today, women only acceded to these positions by inheritance; one inherited a seat on the board either as a surviving spouse or child. Clearly it was by will, and not by willpower. Fortunately, we are no longer in 1976, and fortunately for me, I did not inherit my position, nor am I a CEO yet. My ascension to the position of general manger and my initial orientation to the cosmetics industry are a reflection of many factors. The two most important have been the time frame and the choice of a professional area that strongly corresponded to and reflected my interests.

I entered the business world in the 1970s, a pivotal time for change for women in general. Legislation enabling women to have their own bank accounts appeared in 1966. The 1970s brought the first cabinet-level minister for women's rights, Françoise Giroud. That decade, however, afforded me a possibility by virtue of what it did not offer. Marketing was a relatively uncharted area. In retrospect, selecting this field was all the more surprising given my background. I came from a very traditional family and was given a strong orientation toward my role and my place as a female. Interestingly enough, from the age of six to twelve, I attended a boys' school, the Lycée Jean de Sailly, which counts among its alumni Valéry Giscard-d'Estaing, our former president, and Laurent Fabius, a former prime minister, who happened to be in my class. It was a very competitive environment, and I was confronted with many obstacles, not the least of which was my math teacher, who ignored the few girls in class, who would not reply to our questions, and who dismissed us by telling us that we should be home making jams and jellies. I chose instead to go on for advanced degrees in languages, specializing in Russian. But after rejecting a diplomatic career and finding the work as an international translator difficult, unrewarding, and most importantly, unstimulating, I found myself at a crossroads.

The second factor was my interests. My own creativity led me to my fascination with the cosmetics industry. In short, my own interests and aspirations led me to this very dynamic industry. A friend of mine likes to say that my credentials are a master's from VISA and a doctorate from American Express. I am able to be the consumer in every woman, and that is what drives this industry.

It is no accident that I chose to enter the cosmetics industry. It was, and still is one of the fields where I felt women could advance, at least to a point. So being a woman helped me enter and understand the industry. Cosmetics companies in general, I think, are interested in training women, especially in the marketing area. And that was the direction I personally found most appealing. The beauty industry as a whole is a very marketing-driven business. After spending several years with L'Oréal in France, however, I felt that I was not breaking through to where I wanted to go. I anticipated limitations and was unhappy about them. Typically, French women make lateral moves in business and I wanted to move up. I asked to go abroad, to relocate, more of a male route, if ever there was one. I believe I was the only woman L'Oréal had sent abroad, and to be perfectly honest, the only woman then who had asked to go. The five years that I have spent at our company in New York have enabled me to assimilate the very best of American business practices and attitudes. What may in the past have been demanding or too aggressive behavior is now, I believe, more integrated. For women to have openly admitted their professional ambitions was considered a cardinal sin in France a decade ago, but it certainly does not carry a stigma in New York today.

While women's attitudes may differ somewhat, the determining factor is how women are preparing themselves today to assume roles in management in France. I have been living outside of France for the past five years, and during that time, serious changes have begun to take place. Concerned that I be in a position to reflect properly to you the reality of the present situation, I spoke with the dean of the Institut Supérieur des Affaires, ISA, in Jouy-en-Josas. Véronique de Chantrac, incidentally, is the first woman to have been named as dean of a European business school. She described to me the profile of the female candidates in their MBA program and shared a few statistics.

The program has seen a yearly 2 percent increase in the number of women enrolling since 1985, resulting in a student body that is on average 20 percent female. The average age of these French MBA candidates is between twenty-seven and twenty-eight, and they enter the program already holding advanced degrees as varied as law, philosophy, medicine, and engineering. The consensus is that these women will not allow themselves to be confined to middle management. Having reoriented their careers and made the investment in time for an MBA, they will most likely break through the ranks of middle management a few years down the line.

So much for the capabilities of women today. But what about the attitudes in France toward women in business? To detect these attitudes, we have to look at the norm and the gradual erosion of barriers. Earlier, I mentioned certain professions, such as law and medicine, that have been open to women for over half a century. Strangely enough, in the United States those professions comprised only 5 percent of women as late as 1965. Our country, however, boasts some very distinguished members of both these communities. Simone Weil comes immediately to mind as a lawyer who entered the judiciary and has had a brilliant career in public service. The business community, on the other hand, while not having been so welcoming to women initially, has nonetheless not been hermetically closed to them either. Interestingly, the last bastion, the financial community, is just now being penetrated by women who are attaining positions in corporate finance, management consultancy, and investment banking. Today those doors, which were previously inaccessible, have just begun to swing open. One wonders why it is the revered center of power, i.e., money, has been the last barrier to fall.

Finally, regarding differences in attitudes toward women in business in the United States and in France, I seriously doubt whether global comparisons of attitudes can be made. Perhaps France lends itself to an atmosphere of patronizing women, whereas in the United States, acceptance or tolerance might be the more appropriate description. France's former minister of women's rights, or the condition of women, which is the more literal translation, Françoise Giroud, was quoted years ago as saying that for a woman to be successful in France she simply had to be twice as good as a man. For my part, the more updated version of that would be that one has to work twice as hard to gain acceptance, and always do the very best one can.

BONNET

To explain my experiences as a woman in French business, I will answer four questions: Why did I choose business? Did my family support my decision? Was the education more important because I was a woman? Did the fact that I was a woman influence my employment opportunities? I will also relate an anecdote that reveals the attitude toward women in business, and give a comparative example between the United States and France.

First, why did I choose business? I didn't awake one morning and tell myself that I would be in business and nothing else. But after my *baccalauréat*, the final exam in high school, I knew I wanted to be in the real world. I liked economics and finance, but the university appeared too theoretical and too far removed from life. So I decided to prepare for the entrance examination for HEC, the Ecole des Hautes Etudes Commerciales. My family was very supportive and very proud that I chose a famous school, and they were pleased I did well in the exam. I was naive, because it did not occur to me that business could be more difficult for a woman than for a man. I think my education is responsible for that. My parents never told me that women have more difficulties in certain fields than men. This was a benefit, because then things became a challenge that I wanted to undertake.

I began to feel a little distanced from my girlfriends, who had chosen other fields of study, when I began my "classes préparatoires," which consist of one or two years of study after the *baccalauréat* during which you do nothing but prepare for the entrance examination to a grande école. I was the only female student there. The good thing was that teachers did not treat me any differently. I was surprised, however, when I discovered that as a woman I had to enter a different school, HEC Jeunes Filles, HEC for women, because the real HEC was not open to females at that time. It was fifteen years ago, in 1972, and HEC became coed in 1973, like the other business schools. And now over 40 percent of the students in French business schools are women.

Did the fact that I was a woman influence my employment opportunities? It's difficult to answer, really. I have two different experiences, and I don't think I had special problems because I was a woman. But perhaps unconsciously I chose fields that I knew were more receptive to women. And it's certainly difficult when you want to enter the industry or construction in France.

My first job was not in business. I was hired as a financial expert by the minister of culture to analyze the cultural expenses of cities, departments, and regions. It was the beginning of the decentralization movement in France, and the ministry needed to know the different levels of financial commitment. I had no problem with my contacts with the civil servants I met at the highest levels of responsibility in the local organizations. I had problems when I asked the ministry for a raise. But was it because I was a woman? Was it because the French administration doesn't deal easily with that sort of question? I still can't answer very precisely.

In 1981 I chose to move to the private sector. One of my friends, a journalist in a newspaper group, told me that his group was looking for a person to take over the marketing department of two other publications. I got the job without any difficulty, I must say, because it was a firm where your personal values in life and your skills counted for more than the fact that you were of a given sex. I thought it was great. Two years later I discovered that I was paid 20 percent less than a man having the same level of responsibility. He was in charge of the advertising department, and at that time I had had a big promotion and was in charge of the marketing of all the publications of the group. When I asked why I was paid less, the answer was, "Because you are younger," but the budget I was responsible for was five times his. This anecdote illustrates the fact that one of the concrete problems I experienced in business was the difficulty of getting paid as much as a man. Even when your skill and competence are recognized you have to fight for same salary, even if your level of responsibility is the same. Perhaps it's also because employers—and sometimes women—used to consider a woman's salary as a second salary, which is not true in most cases. But things are changing now. I think young women entering business are really fighting to change this sort of attitude.

I plan to go back to France next year, and I know that I'll have to cope with other problems because I have a child. And I know that I will not escape the well-known dilemma of having to balance family life with the responsibilities of a job. Concerning this, when I was asked to point out the difference between the United States and France, the first thing I thought of was maternity leave. I must say that I was really amazed when I came to the United States five months ago to discover that there was no maternity leave here, in the most modern country in the world. I hope that for American women, that will change soon. In my case, I have taken advantage of the two years nonpaid maternity vacation that a woman can have, which is mandatory in firms employing more than one hundred people.

DIALOGUE

Included here are two comments, especially relevant to the content of the preceding papers, made during the discussion that followed the session on the role of women in French business.

AUDIENCE COMMENT: I was just wondering whether I'd recognize the France I've just left. I've just come to live in the states, and when I lived in France I had to obtain a certificate to practice law in Paris. The person to whom I had to apply was Simone Rozès, who is the highest judge in France. She is obviously a woman who has had an absolutely brilliant career. During the time that I practiced law in France I had the pleasure of working with a large oil company, and the people who used to give me instructions from that company were both women who held important positions in the area of finance. In the banks that I used to work for, some of the more famous nationalized and then denationalized banks, the people who run the international financial part of those banks were women.

It seems to me that perhaps the picture is not quite as it has been presented. The people speaking today have said that there is some form of change happening in France, but I think that it happened really quite a while ago. There are women who not only have positions of responsibility but also succeed in having a family life. The people I was talking about certainly do that. It is, as you know, illegal in France to discriminate on the basis of sex or any other reason. And perhaps the difficulties that some of you have been through present a picture of France which is perhaps not exactly the France that exists now. Perhaps I'm just being naive, I don't know.

AUDIENCE COMMENT: While in France last year, I came across an article in the *Herald Tribune* about one of the top headhunting companies in France. According to the executive from the company, forty out of forty-five companies for whom they did searches in 1985 or 1986 refused to see a woman from the outset. In a whole year, forty out of forty-five searches from the outset screened out women, would not even look at a résumé or hear a name; needless to say, I was shocked to see that.

In addition, I worked in an international organization representing sixty-four countries around the world, and we have several delegates from the United States who've just come back from our annual international conference, attended by approximately 450 delegates. Our organization in the United States tends to be dominated by women, which is somewhat surprising since it's a business and economics organization. There is a presidents' meeting at this international conference which is attended by approximately 130 people. There are two representatives from each country, the president and the president-elect. We have four representatives from the United States because we will be hosting the conference in Boston next year. And so the president and vice president of the committees working on that conference were there. Out of 130 people, there were only seven women, four from the United States, two from Sweden, and one from Finland. When I heard that, I was shocked. Another disturbing element was the reaction to our delegates when they made a presentation. Following the presentation (to men) the response was, "We're surprised that your committee, the International Committee of the United States, has entrusted such a major responsibility to women."

NOTES

1. Unless otherwise indicated, the statistics in this paper are based on: *Tableaux de l'économie Française, édition 1986*, Paris: INSEE, 1986; Nicole Couvi et M. M. Sabot,

Les Femmes et le marché du travail, Paris: Hatier, 1985; and *Femmes en chiffres*, Paris: CNIDF-INSEE, 1986.

2. Jean-Pierre Sereni, "Entreprise: le mur du sexe," *Le Nouvel Economiste* 583 (3/13/87): 16–23.

3. Maryse Huet, "Les Caractéristiques de l'emploi féminin," *Problèmes Economiques* 1928 (6/12/85): 13–17.

4. Christine Mital, "Quand les femmes travaillent, " *Demain, la France*, Paris: L'Expansion, 1986, 385–89.

5. Ibid, p. 385.

6. Gilbert Pointout "Les Femmes Peuvent-elles Occuper toutes les fonctions?" *L'Expansion* (5/25/84–6/7/84):33.

7. Sereni, p. 19.

8. Judith Frommer and M.C. Weitz, "Dominique Dupus, directrice commerciale," *Femmes et Métiers*, Westport: Audio-Forum, 1981.

9. Roselyne Bosch, "Mais comment font-elles?" *Le Point*, 782 (9/14/87): 90–95.

10. Pointout, p. 33.

11. Sereni, p. 19.

12. Ibid.

13. Bosch, p. 91.

14. "Women Make Slow Progress Up the Corporate Ladder," *The Economist* (3/14/87): 61–62.

3

Managers: Education, Recruitment, and Style

Jean-Paul Larçon
Bruno Dufour
Daniel Jouve

LARÇON

Business and management education in France cannot be disassociated from the grandes écoles, elite institutions for specialized study in scientific, business, or literary fields. These schools are comparable in competitiveness and prestige to the Ivy League universities in the United States and fall between the under-graduate and graduate level in education. Although the oldest grandes écoles date back two hundred years, those specializing in business were established over one hundred years ago during the rapid rise of large-scale industry in France; they were located in the principal industrial and commercial centers of the country, such as Marseilles, Bordeaux, Lyons, and of course, Paris. Even today the majority of them depend on the business community and are often run by public regional organizations, like the Chambers of Commerce, which in France are powerful public decentralized agencies generally overseen by a ministry, generally Education and/or Industry.

In the French tradition, the grandes écoles of business emphasized commerce and commercial law, which was considered less noble than engineering; for a long time engineering grandes écoles graduates had much better access to top management positions in French companies. This situation, however, changed radically in the latter half of the 1950s. The French business community faced both the loss of France's colonial empire and the country's entrance into the EEC. These, and other developments, led to a restructuring of business education, particularly the introduction of management science as a course of study. During the 1960s, the case-study method began to replace more traditional teaching approaches, and specialized courses were added. They were taught, in many instances, by professors who had trained in the United States and elsewhere. In twenty years, from 1964–1984, the number of French professors of management went from zero to 2,000. And by the 1970s, the area of management had become an area of advanced research; large sums of money were poured into research laboratories, and doctoral programs were established. Today, these Ph.Ds in marketing, finance, management control, human resources, etc. have become the new professors.

This growth continues. In addition to the four grandes écoles of business, there are independent institutes, and management education is available in certain universities. Altogether, there are thirty schools of management in France, thirteen of which are accredited by the Conférence des Grandes Ecoles. The four grandes écoles produce about 900 graduates a year, with about 2,700 coming from the less selective schools.

Although these institutions are called business schools, a better label would be *diversified management centers*, for they have expanded beyond their original mission. For example, there has been a tremendous boom in educating and training executives. In the United States this is the market of "executive seminars," part of a larger area of continuing education. A masters program specializing in highly important management fields has recently been introduced. At HEC these are international finance, market research, entrepreneurship, and communication. The program lasts a year. In fact, at times the teaching volume that French business schools provide these adults in a short period exceeds the traditional business education young graduates have received. This means, of course, that we must expand our facilities as well, to accommodate this increased demand for training.

The schools compete intensively, of course, first of all to get the best students, but also for money. Because the schools are financed primarily by private enterprise, they must attract and convince companies to fund them; top managers are often called upon to manage fundraising activities. Schools also compete for teachers, recruiting them from all over Europe and America; then the faculty must be encouraged to stay and not join private companies, which can offer much higher salaries.

The schools compete for students, but the students also compete against each other for entrance, going through a particularly severe selection process. There are two principal routes candidates can take. The first is through an "undergraduate" admissions program *(classes préparatoires)*, primarily consisting of economic subjects including many courses in mathematics and statistics. From about 40,000 to 50,000 who attempt to enter this program, only about 8,000 are chosen. Then, for roughly two years, these students prepare for an entrance examination. One out of every three will pass this exam and enter a business school; for the most selective business schools, the figure is one out of ten. The examination consists of many different tests, written and oral; one-third focus on science and mathematics, one-third on foreign languages (two languages, including English), and one-third on general cultural areas, including economics.

The second route to the schools is through "graduate" admission. That is, students with degrees from universities or engineering schools need not attend the *classes préparatoires;* they must, however, pass the examination. And international candidates must fulfill the procedures from their own countries; for example, U.S. students must do well on the Graduate Management Admissions Test (GMAT).

This system is equaled only by the Japanese in severity. It appears elitist and is often criticized for being so. Yet there is a difference: Selection is based strictly on intellectual criteria; age, sex, race, color, nationality, and financial discrimination do not exist.

Those students who enter via the undergraduate admission program spend three years at business school; those who already have a degree spend two. Each year's class has 100–300 students, and there is a high faculty-student ratio. The faculty itself is drawn from representatives of the business world as well as from academic specialists. The educational approach is small work groups in the context of a curriculum based on a work-study experience, with an emphasis on the practical.

The program is designed to balance technical and specialized instruction with basic economics, strategy, and general management courses. Recently, computer-aided learning has increased dramatically, and computer networks have been formed internally and among schools—nationally and internationally. Students choose an area of concentration only in their final year. Today, students favor finance (banking, investment, auditing, and accounting), for that is where salaries are highest; marketing, sales, and advertising (communications); and, like everywhere else, entrepreneurship. Fifteen years ago at HEC, the most popular concentration was public administration; today it is entrepreneurship. In fact, the public administration management area has been discontinued for lack of students. The students' ideal is the small, service-oriented, high tech, venture-capitalized company.

There is a push underway currently to expand business schools. In addition to increasing facilities to accommodate the training and continuing education programs earlier mentioned, there is an increase in the number of students entering the basic program; in HEC this will be an increase of 15–20 percent over the next few years. Further, new schools are opening. Since 1980, one has opened in Nice, in that city's science park. Another has opened in Grenoble; this is a more technically oriented school, for Grenoble is a true high-tech city. A third school opened in Tours.

Graduates are naturally very much in demand, having passed through so many barriers to reach this point. The students at the top schools receive roughly five or six offers each; numerous companies visit the campuses, and competition between them for recruits is intense. Once in place, graduates can aim high:

L'Expansion annually publishes a list of the top one thousand French companies, and 95 percent of their chief executive officers are grandes écoles graduates; 40 percent of these are from the business grandes écoles.

The future everywhere is international, and French business schools are active in promoting a global orientation. This takes several forms. First are the language requirements simply to enter the schools. Second are student exchange programs. For example, 15 percent of HEC's students last year studied abroad at schools like New York University, Berkeley, the University of Michigan, McGill University in Montreal, and the University of British Columbia. In turn, students from these and other schools studied at HEC. The main flow is between France and schools elsewhere in Europe, in North America, and the Pacific.

A final method of internationalizing is by recruiting many foreign students and making our entrance examination available worldwide; already exam centers, set up in more than fifty world capitals, function in connection with the cultural services at the French embassies in these countries. Companies increasingly demand graduates who have skills in various cultures; they look for the flexible and mobile student and can immediately identify someone with the desire and the capability to perform in an international environment. This is why French business schools, even though there is no lack of students in France, are actively seeking brilliant candidates from all over the world. Modern managers will be multicultural and multilingual. An important business school cannot be successful, whether in Europe or the United States, if it remains purely domestic.

Images have a long life. For France as well as for other countries, deeply rooted images may stay alive for a very long time. For France in particular, many changes have occurred since World War II, and these have not always been taken into account by the international community.

To summarize this evolution, a look at changes in France's population structure is revealing. In 1954, 34 percent of the workforce was made up of workers; nearly the same percentage exists today, although more are women. Employees in offices and services (civil servants, bureaucrats, and those in service positions) have grown from 16 percent to 25 percent of the active population. Entrepreneurs decreased from 12 percent to 7 percent, but executives and those in the liberal professions moved from 8 percent to 23 percent, a significant change; farmers decreased from 26 percent to 7 percent, which is also a big change. Comparison with other European countries indicate similarities, with France being between the United Kingdom and Italy in terms of population structure (Exhibit 4). During the past thirty years, France has evolved from a rural country to an urban, industrial country, like all other developed nations.

In years to come, those employed in the services as well as those in the executive ranks will increase. It is envisioned that 80 percent of the GNP will account for those in service, which includes all those not directly involved in the production of goods or in agriculture, as farmers.

Between 1954 and 1983 the rural population moved from the country to the cities, from the farm to the office, because of an increase in the number of civil servants and bureaucrats. Now, as a generation of ex-farmers has settled in the cities, their children are hoping for higher education and more entrepreneurial jobs.

France, in the meantime, is still perceived as the "Three F" country: fashion, food, and fragrance.

Even though much has been said about a "two-speed" France, meaning that if a small part of the population was rapidly changing and driving hard, the remainder was still easy going, the proportion of the very active population is increasing and now significant. The drastic change has fundamentally modified French attitudes, behavior, and value systems. Access to worldwide information, television, and exposure to foreign cultures have accelerated these changes. In addition, because nearly 55 percent of the French own their homes or apartments, they need more money for loans and finance costs. There is, as a consequence, a much more competitive attitude on the job.

Exhibit 4
Employment by Sector

	Germany	France	Italy	United Kingdom	EEC
			Agriculture		
1960	13.8%	22.4%	32.6	4.8%	17.2%
1970	8.5	13.9	20.2	3.3	10.6
1980	5.6	8.7	14.2	2.6	7.3
1983	5.6	8.1	12.4	2.7	6.9
			Industry		
1960	48.2	39.1	33.9	47.6	42.7
1970	49.3	39.7	39.5	44.8	.43.3
1980	44.2	36.0	37.8	37.8	38.3
1983	42.0	33.9	36.0	33.5	35.6
			Services		
1960	38.0	38.5	33.5	47.6	40.1
1970	42.1	46.4	40.3	52.0	46.1
1980	50.3	55.3	47.9	59.6	54.4
1983	54.2	58.0	51.6	63.8	57.5

Printed with permission of Jacques Rojot, Professeur à la Faculté de Droit
et de Sciences Economiques à l'INSEAD

VALUE SYSTEMS AND CULTURAL DIFFERENCES

France is considered a Latin country but is, in fact, a real melting pot. Through the centuries, invaders from the east, north, and south have combined to form a true blend of European civilizations. No country in Europe has such a variety of components. And the persistence of minority groups like Bretons, Basques, Corsicans, and even Savoyards in seeking autonomy shows that this mosaic is still alive. Current problems with immigrants from Spain, Portugal, and particularly North Africa indicate that the French are still preoccupied with the issue, which is even a part of political debate.

Despite this mixture, however, the basic French value system remains closer to that of Latin countries than to Anglo-Saxon ones. Louis XIV's revocation of the Edict of Nantes in the seventeenth century is a true indication of this value system. Rejecting Protestant ideology, the king established such Latin values as a strong dependence on spiritual authority and temporal authority, and strong dependence regarding money, time, family, and work.

In France, as in most Latin countries, the tradition is that God is difficult to reach and to communicate with. An intermediary, like a priest, is needed: Someone—a man—has received this power of intermediation. Self-confession is of no value, nor is self-approval. It is no wonder, then, that the relations with temporal authority are cut from the same cloth. Political powers are centralized, remote, and somewhat mythical. Power comes from position, not from competence.

In families, the eldest son is a "me-too" father, and there is no egalitarianism between brothers and sisters. Latin families are highly centralized under the domination of grandparents. Until after World War II, many families lived together under the same roof. *L'esprit de famille* was a strong leitmotiv, not only to manage family problems, but family businesses. Hiring was related to kinship more than to competence.

The grandes écoles were another type of *grande famille* system, with kinship replaced by a very selective entrance exam. Relation to authority had the same value as relation to knowledge: Very few people had the power—the knowledge—and could transmit it to some happy few. In this system, relation to time was the relationship to God's time, so long-term projects were more important than short-term issues and methods. Problem-finding was more important than problem-solving; objectives were more important than implementation; time considerations were irrelevant. In such a system, money was seen as the devil's invention and not as a useful tool. Work was necessary and compulsory; the world *travail* is derived from the Latin *tripalium,* which was an instrument of torture. The etymological root of the Anglo-Saxon word *work* is *erg,* which also appears in *energy* and *org*anization, so that "work" is closer to the concept of human force or energy. In the Anglo-Saxon value system, as Max Weber described it, relation to authority, time, money, and family is completely different.

These relationships are traditionally more balanced, and individual autonomy is much more important. Political systems are federal, not centralized. Even though France defined the concepts *Liberté, Egalité, Fraternité*, the revolution replaced an aristocratic power by a bureaucratic one. *Plus ça change et plus c'est la même chose*. People had changed but the system was nearly the same! (An example of this is France's continued unwillingness to invest in a more egalitarian system of higher education. France ranks eleventh in OECD countries in terms of educational investment, which indicates this is not a high priority.)

The values that make up the culture of French companies are very different from those in the Anglo-Saxon world. As a result, French small and medium-sized firms are managed completely differently from American ones. But the French style of management will be affected as the population changes.

COMPARISONS BETWEEN FRENCH AND AMERICAN COMPANIES

Thirty years ago, the typical French small family business would have been established under a limited responsibility incorporation statute (S.A.R.L.). No one beyond suppliers or bankers could have reliable information on its status, finances, or decisions. To ensure that no information would leak out, the owner would try to hire members of his immediate family.

Usually, the first generation strove hard to get the business going. The second would also work hard to develop the company; but with the third generation of cousins came the habits of a good standard of living and no real motivation to work together. Very few companies could survive the third or fourth generations. Spending was high; profits as well as efficiency were low. Very few people had higher education or strong experience outside the job.

Because of the typically large size of Latin families, by the third generation more than ten people from the same family could be in the same business; in some cases, by the fourth or fifth generation, capital could be divided among eighty family partners, which meant coming to decisions about investment or objectives was difficult. As family considerations prevailed and competition was irrelevant, profitability would decrease; hence the power of negotiation with customers or suppliers diminished. Undercapitalized because of poor economic results and the family's desire to take too much from the company, this small or medium-sized business would fall into the hands of bankers. Strategic plans, much less budgets, did not exist.

So that everyone in the family would be satisfied, opportunism was the rule, which encouraged people to start small new ventures inside the company. Dispersion, lack of synergy and coherence, and lack of management all made things difficult for such firms. The tremendous shortage of goods following the war enabled these companies to survive in a demanding economy with a low competition profile. Eventually, however, the absence of flexibility because of an unwillingness to consider market environment and competition meant these firms were blocked. They could not try new approaches, audit their primary activities, or export.

The recent economic crisis and the advent of global competition along with the drastic changes in management tools were a tremendous shock for this kind of business. Only the ones that could adapt survived; most became bankrupt, many vanished. And this was not only true for small and medium-sized companies; huge, inflexible companies with nearsighted strategy, like those in steel or mining industries, were also affected. Large staffs had to become leaner and more aggressive. Those with financial reserves could survive, but others were raided by holding companies.

Slowly but surely France has deindustrialized, moving toward services, which require fewer investments and can develop more rapidly. We have moved into new businesses like biotechnology, aerospace, nuclear energy, and other high-tech areas; industrialists moved out of classic, basic industries like automobiles, consumer appliances, and mechanical equipment.

Nonetheless, France has lacked qualified manpower because no one cares about training: Neither companies nor the national education system are responsible for this important area. In Germany, firms invest in on-the-job training, using modern equipment, so large companies train twice the personnel they need. This provides the rest of the industry, and the industrial community overall, with the qualified work force they need.

Tools such as microcomputers, which imply that people manage their own information systems, are more autonomous and more willing to perform, and the fact that competition is more positively viewed have forced companies to adapt. Management styles have changed. The sense of responsibility is more shared than it was before, and competence has replaced *l'esprit de famille*. Individualism has increased, and short-term profits are more important. Strategic planning has developed, and management training is becoming a growth industry in the service sector. Employees as a result are more mature and need less authority, hence are closer to decision making.

The role of trade unions has also changed, and the French political environment has influenced that. France's largest union, the CGT, has declined; its membership has dropped 50 percent in the past ten years.

POLITICAL ENVIRONMENT

Recent political events in France have created a unique situation. When the Socialists came to power in 1981, they took a dogmatic approach. They soon discovered, however, that it was impossible to govern France without recognizing the European and international environment, for economic as well as social reasons. A year and a half later, Prime Minister Mauroy made a complete U-turn, adjusting to a more classic economic approach that encompassed budget and financial considerations.

Suddenly, the Socialists discovered that businesses and companies had to be cared for and that France dramatically needed entrepreneurship. By the end of 1983, nationalizations had been costly, and replacement of complete management teams in these companies had been catastrophic. The heavy financial losses these new managers faced and the amount of unemployment the companies experienced were responsible for much of the Socialists' change of direction. Beginning in August 1983, the government moved from a demand-supported economy that, through distribution of buying power, had created much import activity, to a more classic, balanced economy. It discovered that large companies were generally firing as many people as small and medium-sized companies would hire.

Meanwhile, French unions, most of which are related to political parties, were tied up in controversy. Their historical background, the 1906 Charte d'Amiens, was based on the concept of anarchosyndicalism. They hoped, therefore, that with a leftist government in power, unionism would grow quickly. In fact, the opposite occurred. With Socialists in the government, nearly 10 percent of the total unionized work force disengaged from trade unions. The traditional objectives of trade unions revolved around class warfare, and their battles had in fact been won; there were no more reasons for staying in the unions. Few unions had focused on negotiating work conditions, the day-to-day struggles, but had instead been interested in gaining power. This is typical of long-term, traditional French or Latin objectives.

In this new, unusual situation, the French learned how to worship business values, a change that accompanied training for nonunionized workers. In areas like private schooling or transportation, France encountered large demonstrations by those opposing socialist dogmatism. Over one million people demonstrated against the Socialists on the private school issue, and the strike, organized by small and medium-sized trucking businesses against the Ministry of Transportation, was a clear message to the government from the silent majority—among which were members of the Socialist electorate.

The 1986 elections brought a balance of power, with a Socialist president and a rightist prime minister, a situation that many feared would provoke a civil war. Some left the country to establish businesses elsewhere; others had left in 1981 and 1982 anticipating a total Socialist failure. As it turned out, neither flight nor fight was the solution. The failure of the nationalizations prepared France for denationalization. The new weakness of trade unions liberated entrepreneurs, allowing them to hire and fire much more easily than in the past. Leftist dogmatism canceled rightist dogmatism, and cohabitation became a process in which everyday problems had to be solved without worrying about a long-term doomsday philosophy. This period can be seen as training in controversy, allowing people from both political sides to understand the situation much more realistically.

Most French realized that things had changed for good. Never before had a French government, much less one with a Socialist president, done so much to foster company profits and export policies. But extensive damage had been inflicted by previous governments, most of them nonleftist, which had considered

French firms as the economic cash cow of the nation. All kinds of taxes and social charges and other fiscal gimmicks had already been invented by pre-Socialist governments.

The enduring philosophy of optimizing both the economic and social aspects of French life had revealed its costs and limits; France realized that the economy had to take precedence. Said one government leader, "When the pie is too small, there is nothing to share."

Now newspapers and other media became filled with economic news: currency rates, inflation rates, GNP, exports, trade balance figures—all kinds of economic ratios were displayed. The Paris stock exchange rose as it never had before; prices were to double in a year, with a 40 percent increase on a yearly average. France discovered that money was not an evil invention but something to work with. By the end of 1987, the situation had returned to normal, after passing through an abnormal period in which stocks had been overpriced.

Nonetheless, the nation's apprenticeship had been accomplished; never had management values been so praised, which created a strong demand for management training throughout French businesses. Because management education in France had dealt with drastic changes in the past twenty years, French business schools and other institutions could answer that demand.

THE FRENCH BUSINESS EDUCATION SYSTEM

Before 1968, French higher education in the management field was rather rudimentary, although the grandes écoles system had a highly selective entrance procedure, and the Chamber of Commerce provided a rather pragmatic approach to teaching business topics.

Many business schools had been founded in the nineteenth century or early twentieth century, but as late as the 1970s the study of functional areas of management or of subjects like macro- or microeconomics was neglected. Research was almost unknown, as was the case-study method. Marketing was just appearing in the curriculum. Business policy, management, organizational behavior, international business, computer science, and the like were not on the menu.

From 1969 to 1975, however, a very intensive upgrading took place. This led to the institution of full-time faculties, research centers, continuing education centers, advanced degree programs, international programs, and international networks and exchanges. Standards rose as a result of competition. New tools and approaches were designed; investments were made in modern buildings, computers, and language labs. Management education became a capital-intensive business. The race was on to make these schools as good as other famous international business schools, a process taking place mostly in private or semi-private graduate business institutions.

During this period, many schools moved to new campuses outside big cities and began to build up full-time teaching staffs. New reforms accompanied new curricula. For example, the Continuing Education Act of 1971 made it mandatory for companies to spend 1 percent of salaries plus social charges on training. In the 1980s, companies began funding faculty chairs, entrepreneurship, and other business education programs.

The future will bring further development in both the quality and the range of activities found in French business education. The increasing demand for business graduates—six offers per graduate—means increased quality as well. Many American business schools have discovered this new fast-growth market in France. These new challenges call for imagination, for there is no clear model of a truly "European" higher education system in management.

Accompanying France's discovery of management is the elevation of some business people to the status of stars, for example, Mr. Lagardère of Matra, Mr. Bouygues, and Mr. Bernard Tapie, whose communication skills assure him large audiences. Television and radio now all have economic and business programs that feature business people and companies prominently.

Perhaps this is just a new craze in France. But the general feeling is that something has changed in the value system because there have been changes in the components of that value system.

CONCLUSION

We may encounter in the years to come a slight backlash regarding entrepreneurial values—a small pendulum effect—but even with a volatile stock market, there has been no sign of one. Unionism, however, might stage a slight comeback.

The major challenge to business and business education will arrive with the creation of a single internal market in Europe by 1992. The economy has changed, and we expect that the service sector will increase from 60 percent to 80 percent of the total workforce. This means new jobs and new services must be created; competition strengthens each day. Newer and higher technologies are infusing all jobs; better communications are required, along with flexibility. Companies must become "pluricultural," more adaptable to new challenges.

Changes will have to occur in the traditional educational system in France on the primary and secondary levels. These are the last conservative bastions; the rest of the country has changed. Because the French Ministry of Education is highly centralized, with more than one million employees in its bureaucracy, there is not much to hope for beyond a total regionalization of the education system, as occurred in Germany.

Companies will have to continue to adapt and spend more money to train people instead of getting them from the French national education system. It will take another ten years before French high schools can really change, and experience in other developed countries suggests that high school systems are difficult to manage. Nevertheless, values are no longer transmitted by the national education system; rather, they arrive via television and other media, the family, and other experiences like summer jobs, and the development of individual initiatives.

JOUVE

When we set out to discover what the new generation of French executives looks like, we run into a basic problem: The concept of *executive* does not exist in France. We have the word *cadre* (literally, frame), and there are about three million of them in the country. [Originally, *cadre* referred to anyone with managerial responsibility. A *cadre moyen* was the equivalent of an American in middle management, a manager, while a *cadre supérieur* was an executive.] My secretary, for example, is a *cadre;* she is not, however, an executive. The French have tried to sort out various *cadres*: there are *cadres supérieurs* and the *cadres moyens*. But here as elsewhere there is inflation. Everyone wants to be a *cadre supérieur* or *cadre moyen*. So the term *cadre dirigeant* was forged to cover executive. (Now, too many people want to be *cadre dirigeant*.) I do not like the word *cadre* because it is something static, something you put on the wall and it hangs there for a few hundred years. For me, the term *executive* refers to the people who manage the company, the "number ones," the captains and generals—and these are the subjects of the following discussion, which not only explores changes in French executives but compares these people with, primarily, their American counterparts. We begin by asking: Where do French executives come from?

BACKGROUND

There is nothing very surprising about the origins of French executives: Most have a father who was also an executive. I did a survey five years ago of the chief executives of the 1,000 largest French companies. It showed that chief executives tend to come from families where the father was a businessman; very few were the sons or daughters of farmers or civil servants despite the size of these populations. As for their education, they are usually graduates of the grandes écoles. This system of schools, some of which date back to the eighteenth century, is one of the foundations of France and a source of pride. Traditionally the grandes écoles were dedicated to training engineers, but in the last thirty to forty years, the engineering schools (Polytechnique, Centrale, Arts et Métiers, and Supaéro) have been joined by a group of business schools: HEC, ISA, ESSEC, and the Ecole Supérieure de Commerce de Paris and its equivalents in other major cities. These business schools operate with the same exceptionally high standards as their engineering counterparts. Three other schools that produce some of France's outstanding executives are the Ecole Normale Supérieure, the Institut d'Etudes Politiques, and the Ecole Nationale d'Administration, whose graduates, though trained for government service, often end up in the business sector. As has been true in the past, the grandes écoles today still turn out France's best executives.

Nonetheless, I believe we are witnessing a big change in these graduates' attitudes. As one writer puts it, they are going from the *bof* (indifferent) generation to the *boss* generation; they're interested in business, they want to start companies. They like money and want to make—if possible—big money.

This is something new, and I think this attitude will become even more pervasive in the future. As evidence, I can provide an example from the Institut d'Etudes Politiques, my alma mater. This school is unique because students can choose between two programs, one in the area of public service, and the other in economy and finance, to prepare for careers in either government or business. This year, for the first time in the school's 115-year history, more students are studying to go into business than government. Today, French people no longer want to be civil servants; they want to be in business, and this is a revolution.

Unfortunately, this new enthusiasm for business does not always guarantee an awareness of the realities of business. It has become, for example, quite fashionable for the younger generation to want to start a business. It has also become something of a joke. Newspapers report that two twenty-one-year-old graduates are setting up a company to compete with Coca-Cola. There are photographs, interviews, hoopla; a week later they go bankrupt, but this is rarely mentioned. On the whole, the media tend to overplay such stories and give the impression that more is happening than really is. The new generation's admiration for someone like Mr. Bernard Tapie is another sign that it lacks sound judgment. Mr. Tapie buys the assets of bankrupt companies for one franc. It is very hard to lose money with such an approach, so he appears to be very successful. Of course, his days are numbered, but in the meantime he is, unfortunately, a role model for young people, who will be very disappointed when they realize he is another big joke.

INTERNATIONALIZATION

I receive many letters from young Americans asking me to help them find a job in Paris. I have to tell them it is becoming more and more difficult to do that because American companies have realized that instead of paying American executives hardship allowances to live in Paris, they can hire French executives for half the price. Nor do we find many high-level executives from other European countries, although one would think the Common Market would encourage this. Of course, there are examples of foreign executives who work in French companies: The future chief executive of L'Oréal is an Englishman; the vice president of marketing at Peugeot is an American who used to work for Ford, which may explain why Peugeot is selling more cars. In a slightly different context, the consortium that builds Airbus—a joint French, German, Spanish, and British venture—is managed chiefly by executives from France and Germany and is an amazing example of how executives from different countries can work together productively. Another joint effort is GE's collaboration with the French company SNECMA to build the CFM56 jet engines, a highly successful program headed by a Frenchman. Overall, however, the number of foreign executives in French companies is very small.

Regarding women executives: Ten years ago women decided they wanted to be executives, and if they are not running everything today, it is only because they haven't been at it long enough.

But we can lose executives, and some of the best. Five years ago the government passed a law concerning early retirement that was a very serious mistake. The idea was to retire people at age fifty-five to create jobs for people who were twenty-one. The result was that many very smart people who really could have helped create jobs for young people ended up growing roses on the Riviera. A story about Aérospatiale, the French partner in Airbus Industrie, illustrates this well.

The new chairman of Aérospatiale became concerned when he saw that delays in designing the wings for the new model Airbus were holding up the entire program, and he arranged a meeting with those in charge of the project. The next day, two twenty-four-year-old engineers, fresh from school, arrived in his office.

"You're in charge of this important project?" he asked in disbelief. "What happened to the experienced engineers who used to be here?"

"Oh, they were forced to take early retirement," he was told.

When the chairman called the company's general secretary and insisted that he wanted the engineers rehired, he was told that according to the new law, the company did not have the right to do that. Furious, he told the general secretary that he would talk to the prime minister or the president if he had to; he would even break the law, but he wanted those people back on that project the following week. A few days later, the chairman found the general secretary waiting for him.

"So, where are they?" said the chairman. "I told you I wanted them back."

"Well," came the reply, "they're in Seattle, working for Boeing."

French executives have a fascination with the United States. They believe that everything American is better and more efficient. Often they are right, although such faith in the "American Way" can be carried to absurd lengths, for example, slipping English terms into their speech to appear more up-to-date. This fascination, I believe, reflects a great and important change in attitude: French executives are willing to work abroad and enjoy doing so. The French used to be like peasants, wanting to stay close to home. They wanted to live in Paris—in the right sections of Paris. But they have come to realize that working for a time in a foreign country can boost their careers.

Naturally, working in the United States is desirable; it's prestigious. A secretary takes pride in saying that the boss is traveling in the United States. London is popular with bankers and financiers, not because of its weather or food, but because its tax system is very favorable to non-British workers. Asia has traditionally attracted a small group of French expatriates, many of whom are so seduced by its culture that they settle there permanently. On the other hand, there are places French executives do not want to go—Saudia Arabia, for example, because of its strict Moslem culture, or Africa. When executives accept such assignments, the reason is usually because their living allowance enables them to save their entire salary.

The timing of this period abroad can be a problem. The typical young French executive likes the idea of going abroad to work soon after he or she graduates, but an employer usually prefers that there first be some knowledge of the company, its products, and procedures. "Wait five years," the executive is told, "and then we'll send you to Hong Kong." But five years later the executive is married to a lawyer working in Paris; they have two children, and the prospect of going to Hong Kong is considerably less attractive.

Regardless of where they go or for whom they work, these expatriate French executives tend to have one thing in common: They invariably come back to France. Perhaps their children are about to enter high school; perhaps they are very attached to their country. Whatever the reasons, the result is that France does not suffer the "brain drain" that other countries like Great Britain do.

The attitude toward working in the provinces is also changing. Twenty years ago, living and working outside Paris implied a not very stimulating environment, but this is no longer true. There are exciting things going on in most of France's largest cities, which means that people are much more willing to move there. Once again, the problem is with two-career families. If both spouses have good jobs in Paris and one is offered an interesting opportunity in another city, it is unlikely the other will also find something suitable there. Consequently, they remain in Paris.

ON AND OFF THE JOB

French executives have traditionally been attracted to jobs in finance. You are in an office, dealing with the government sector, and can move back and forth between the government and business sectors easily, whether the job is in banking or corporate finance. Production, however, has never been very appealing. With the exception of the Ecole des Arts et Métiers, whose graduates have a real interest in factories and manufacturing, the major engineering schools have turned out executives who have no interest in doing the job they were trained to do. As factories become more modern, more automated, and cleaner, however, attracting these grandes écoles graduates—who never liked getting their hands dirty—into production will become easier.

Other fields are gaining popularity as well, for example, human resources management. Previously, companies were satisfied to place a retired army colonel or someone who had been a complete failure in every other field in charge of this function. In the past twenty years, however, this position has become more important, and today, the person who fills it sits on the five- or six-member management committee. Now every company wants a good head of human resources, but finding one is not simple. Because twenty-five years ago smart people were not going into this field, there is today a shortage of seasoned executives to draw from. But as the responsibilities, rewards, and potential of the job increase—a head of human resources can now move up to chief executive—so will the number of talented managers.

Another fashionable area is communications. Every company also wants a good director of communications. Because it is a relatively new field, there are problems similar to those found in human resources: not many good people available. Unlike human resources, however, where years of experience and some grey hair is helpful, in communications, people can be trained much faster.

The sales function, of course, remains the most difficult area. People in France think selling is degrading, imagining the *tireur de sonnette*, the guy who pulled the old doorbell cord to sell brooms. They have yet to realize that the doorbell is now electric and selling has become a highly sophisticated activity. This problem is so critical that when some companies hire recent graduates, they ask them to sign an agreement to work in sales at the start of their careers; otherwise, the company knows the new people will refuse to do it. This dislike for sales naturally carries over into customer relations. In the failure to meet delivery schedules, for example, it is common to hear, "Well, the French product is better, but they don't deliver on time, so we're going elsewhere." The same is true for poor after-sales service: The French may make better machine tools than the Germans and may sell them at a lower price, but they still have trouble competing because the Germans take post-sale service seriously, and the French do not.

French executives who are graduates of the grandes écoles have tended to be arrogant, and this is not a quality that is disappearing. Nor do modern French executives seem to be less emotionally sensitive about work than their predecessors. In the United States, two executives can argue about something and neither feels rejected or hurt if the other does not agree with a point of view. In France, if one executive tells another he does not agree with him it means "you don't love me." This is a big problem: If things are to run smoothly, executives must also be diplomats.

Another trait that has not changed is the French reluctance to talk about money. During the past ten years I have interviewed some 6,000 executives. I ask them to tell me about their careers, education, and experiences, and they are pleased to do so. I have yet to meet one who told me how much money he made before I asked that question.

An important change that has taken place is the relationship between company executives and other employees. A long-standing tradition in France is that employees hate their boss and others running the company. But a lot of companies have gone bankrupt, and many people have lost their jobs. If a company is doing well, its employees now recognize that the executives have probably been doing a good job. They respect these executives and want them to be well paid so they will stay. This is an attitude that has never existed in France before.

French executives work very hard. Contrary to tales about lax working habits and morning wine breaks, these people, especially the ones at the top, often carry an unreasonably large share of the workload in French companies, a problem I shall mention subsequently. French executives, when we take a look at their zealously protected private lives, do not have the time for many extra-professional activities.

More executives jog or play tennis than in the past, as France, like the United States, has become preoccupied with physical fitness. They also travel abroad for pleasure more than in the past, though unfortunately the objective is just that, pleasure, rather than learning more about the countries they are visiting—beyond noting that the food is not as good as in France and that the women are not as well dressed, of course.

STRENGTHS AND WEAKNESSES

A word that the French love to use to irritate Americans is *culture*. If someone wants to attend a top French engineering school, he or she needs to excel in mathematics; but many people are good in mathematics, so there has to be another area of excellence, like French literature, if that person wants to be accepted. And by graduation, students have gained not only a strong engineering background, but a solid general culture as well. These people *are* cultured. They love books, they love ideas, and they love to talk about them. Executives at General Motors may be very good at building cars—or at least they used to be—but French executives will certainly be more stimulating and entertaining company over dinner.

There are many illustrations of this. Pierre Barret entered HEC, the leading French business school, and promptly left when he was not elected president of the student union; he went off to fight in the Algerian war and returned to the school two years later, in 1961, having received the Legion of Honor for military heroism. He has since run a large advertising firm, managed *L'Express*, a leading French magazine, and been president of Europe 1, a major radio station. In addition, he is a professional motorcycle racing champion and has a solid reputation as the author of works on the Middle Ages. Then there is Jacques Mayoux, the former president of Société Générale. People who worked for him several years ago when he was the head of a steel company have told me how amazed they were when, after a hard day's work, he would sit in his office and deliver lectures on fourteenth-century Germany or the flooding of the Yang-Tse-Kiang in the nineteenth century or recite page after page of Cervantes. Another example is Arnaud de Vitry, who graduated in the top of his class at Harvard Business School and turned his second-year thesis into a company of which he has been a board member since age twenty-five. The company, of course, is Digital

Equipment Corporation. Almost as remarkable, he uses his DEC computer to organize his library of books on the science of perspective, the largest such collection in the world. These are but a few executives among many of whom we are proud and who, I believe, set France apart from other countries.

Unfortunately, these exceptional people rarely get involved in politics. In 1980, even before the Socialist majority in Parliament, I was told by a deputy that when discussions about what to do with a company going bankrupt took place, only five deputies out of five hundred could read a balance sheet and understand what it meant; the others had no idea how a company really worked. Some executives do feel a duty to bring their experience, common sense, and efficiency to politics—Mr. Bousquet, the founder of Cacharel is a member of Parliament—but these are exceptions, and we need more people of their caliber in the nation's political life.

There are, I believe, two major problems in France today regarding executives. First, there are not enough outstanding executives. The grandes écoles still turn out about the same number of graduates as they did fifty years ago. I think they could double their output without lowering the quality of education. Second, although we are good at selecting and educating exceptional people, we are not good in dealing with average people, those who do not get into the best schools. These people fill the middle management level, which is the weakest echelon in French companies. They feel that their chances of reaching the top are slim because they have not attended the right school, which is sad because some have the potential. As a result, they become demotivated, indifferent, and bitter; their aim is to get through the year as painlessly as possible and then take a vacation at Club Med. Their scholastic, professional, and social status are not visible because they wear swimsuits, and money does not matter because it is replaced by beads. I would argue that Club Med is really an outgrowth of this malaise among middle managers.

There is much talk of training these people. Unfortunately, both the politicians and the companies talk in terms of money rather than quality. The sums spent are indeed significant, since companies are legally required to allocate a certain amount each year to training; but the training itself is generally poor because it is not administered by high-caliber people. Thus, someone who is handicapped at the start because of a mediocre education remains handicapped because of mediocre training. He will continue to think it doesn't matter what kind of job he does, for he has no chance of advancement. This attitude marks a big difference between France and the United States, and we must do something to change it.

One solution is to use the company's own top executives as teachers in the company's middle management training programs instead of calling on professional trainers. This would provide middle managers the quality of training they missed by not attending one of the best schools. Top executives would benefit, for they would be able to shift some of their excessive workload onto these better qualified and harder working middle managers.

DIALOGUE

QUESTION: Are there examples of French companies with a better reputation for training people? Companies that are more receptive to new ideas?

JOUVE: It's very simple: All the U.S. multinationals in France—IBM, Proctor & Gamble, and so on. They have no prejudice toward somebody who has no school degree. A lot of people have become very good executives because they worked for ITT or Ford or IBM. And if you are a young Frenchman and you don't have a fancy diploma, my advice is to go to work for an American company. And then, later on, you can go somewhere else.

QUESTION: Can you point out French companies that have recognized the need to improve that kind of training?

JOUVE: Yes. In my book I interviewed a man who is the head of human resources for DMC, a textile company. He was hired by Mr. Charlier, who became chief executive five years ago when the company was on the verge of bankruptcy. By getting rid of deadwood, attracting new people, and by training and developing the talent already in the company, the two managed to turn the situation around. They also instituted a performance appraisal system that works, no small feat given the difficulty of convincing a French executive to rate people who work for him fairly and openly. In general, however, U.S. companies do this better.

QUESTION: You mentioned that the European executive, French executives, are fascinated by the American way, but do you find they are equally fascinated by the Japanese way?

JOUVE: No, not at all. I went to Japan only once but I'm not impressed. Some people just work harder and that's not impressive. We try to have people work smarter. A lot of sectors of Japanese industry are so backward and so inefficient, it's unbelievable. But they end up producing so many cars you end up thinking they must be doing something right. But the French are not that impressed or fascinated by the Japanese.

QUESTION: Regarding careers, how well accepted is it to go from one company to another?

JOUVE: I would say that today in France there is a very strong difference between people under forty-five and over forty-five. People over forty-five are critical of changing companies; for those under forty-five, France is like any country in the world. You call up somebody, you say you are an executive recruiter and you have a job he may be interested in, and the answer is the same as in Boston, New York, or Atlanta: "Let me close my door."

QUESTION: It appears the hope for sales and marketing is with the new generation. However, you still have people between fifty and fifty-five who are still there and in no rush to step aside. How frustrating do young people find this?

JOUVE: This is not the frustration of young people. The problem is not with marketing. People love marketing. The problem is with sales: No one wants to sell. You have a little briefcase and you have to go out and get orders and then get the guy to send the orders. And if you come back at night without any orders, it hurts and you feel like a bad student. People have been trained to think they should strive for perfection, and they don't want to make any mistakes. A story about export sales makes this point. When a French executive goes to Australia on a sales trip, he always flies Air France, so he never meets his clients or competitors, who fly other airlines. And the first thing he does when he arrives in Australia is confirm his return flight. The German, however, has an open return, and the Japanese has no return ticket at all.

QUESTION: How do you prepare the French executives for this tremendous change of culture, different ways of looking at business? Is it strictly a matter of sending them to the United States?

JOUVE: I don't think there are many middle managers who are sent to work in the States unless on limited projects, for example, technicians for limited periods of time. There are not too many training programs for that. But you have to realize that they all watch French TV and most French TV programs are American programs, so they know very well how Americans live. They see it on TV every day.

I think it's true the culture of the business community is different, but it's simpler, so they grasp very quickly what's important. If you are a controller and you are supposed to send your figures on the second day of the month at noon, it doesn't take long to know that it's not at one o'clock—or, in a French company sometime between now and the end of the week—and they learn that very fast because the signals are clear and the goals are very simple. It's the bottom line. They like it or they don't like it, they stay longer or leave, but they understand very well what the rules are.

In conclusion, I would state that I have great admiration for many of our executives in France and hope that others would recognize their abilities. And what is the best way to become a top French executive? Those who run French business schools will say that the best way is to get a liberal arts education in the United States and then study business in France. I believe my way was better: to study liberal arts in France and get business training in America.

Appendix I

Chronology of Key Political and Economic Events

1936   Electoral victory of the Socialist Popular Front

Major social legislation enacted: paid vacations, eight-hour day, collective bargaining

1937   Nationalization of the railroads and the creation of the SNCF (Société Nationale des Chemins de Fer Français)

1938   Socialist Popular Front government falls

1939   Military mobilization of France

1940   German troops enter Paris

General de Gaulle, in London, calls for resistance

Pétain government signs armistice with Germany

Vote of Vichy government establishes the French state

General de Gaulle is sentenced to death in absentia

Trade unions abolished

1942   Allies land in North Africa; Germans move into unoccupied France

1944   Allied landings in Normandy

Liberation of Paris

Female suffrage enacted

Government seizes Renault for collaboration with Germany

Nationalization of coal mines

1945   Nationalization of Renault

Legislation creates company work councils (*comités d'entreprise*)

German army capitulates

National health insurance (*sécurité sociale*) created

General de Gaulle confirmed as head of the government

Nuclear energy commission created (CEA)

Bank of France and main deposit banks nationalized

1946   General de Gaulle resigns

Planning Commission created under Jean Monnet

Gas and electricity industries nationalized

Thirty-four insurance companies nationalized

Law granting state allowances for large families enacted

Constitution of the Fourth Republic approved by referendum

Fourth Republic hold first elections

1947   First Plan, to modernize France, enacted

Communist ministers dismissed from the government

Newly formed Gaullist party (RPF) gains 40 percent of municipal elections

Force Ouvrière (FO) created in a split with the CGT, the Communist trade union

1948   Marshall Plan adopted

1949   France ratifies NATO Treaty

1951   Treaty creating the European Coal and Steel Community (CECA) signed

Statutory minimum wage (SMIG) created

1954   Geneva accords on armistice in Vietnam

Nationalist insurrection in Algeria begins

Numerous collective bargaining agreements signed

1956   Law granting a third week paid vacation enacted

1957   Treaty of Rome establishing the European Economic Community (EEC) signed

1958   Insurrection of French settlers in Algeria

Committee formed to demand that General de Gaulle be returned to power

General de Gaulle government formed

Constitution of the Fifth Republic approved by referendum

General de Gaulle becomes president

A new currency, the new Franc, is created

1961   Six Common Market countries adopt common import duties

Attempted coup of French generals in Algeria; the army remains loyal to de Gaulle

1962   Cease-fire agreement for Algeria

Georges Pompidou becomes prime minister

Independence for Algeria approved by referendum

Amendment to the constitution introducing the popular election of the president, accepted by referendum

Renault grants employees a fourth week paid vacation

1965   General de Gaulle reelected president

1966   France leaves NATO and demands the withdrawal of all foreign troops
stationed on her territory

First nuclear reactor installed

1967   Profit-sharing legislation enacted

Second nuclear reactor installed

1968   The "May events": student demonstrations, mass strikes

"Accords de Grenelle" settle the strikes
—35% increase in the minimum wage
—increased protection for labor unions
—promise of paying workers on a monthly rather than hourly basis

Massive Gaullist victory in parliamentary elections

Custom barriers between the six EEC countries eliminated

1969   Agreement on job security signed between CNPF
(employers' union, Conseil national du patronat français) and trade unions,
setting conditions for layoffs

Constitutional referendum defeated; General de Gaulle resigns as president

Law granting a fourth week paid vacation enacted

Georges Pompidou elected president, Jacques Chaban-Delmas becomes prime
minister, and Valéry Giscard d'Estaing becomes minister of finances

Plan of economic austerity adopted: credit control and price freeze instituted

1970   EEC enters final phase of unification with its own budget and independent
financial resources; financing for the Common Agricultural Policy adopted

Collective bargaining agreements between the employers association, the
CNPF, and the trade unions concerning maternity leave, training, and a
salaried status for all employees

General de Gaulle dies

Airbus Industrie, a consortium of French, German and Dutch companies,
created

Eight nuclear reactors in operation

Social transfer payments as a percent of GDP: 19.3 percent

1971   François Mitterrand elected head of the French Socialist Party

1972   Socialists, Communists, and Left Radicals sign an electoral coalition, the
Common Program of government

Price freeze for fifty-four industries, representing twelve percent of
production, ends

Pierre Messmer becomes prime minister, Jacques Chirac minister of
agriculture and Valéry Giscard d'Estaing remains minister of finance

First women admitted to Polytechnique, the grande école for civil servants

1973   Denmark, Ireland, and the United Kingdom enter the EEC

Month-long strikes at Renault

OPEC restricts oil production, resulting in worldwide shortages and price increases

Adoption of an anti-inflation program

Annual inflation: 7.3 percent; unemployment 1.9 percent

1974   Strikes of bank employees

Jacques Chirac becomes Minister of the Interior

Death of President Georges Pompidou

Valéry Giscard d'Estaing elected president; Gaullist Jacques Chirac becomes prime minister

Vote granted to eighteen-year-olds

Adoption of anti-inflation and energy-saving programs

Annual inflation: 13.7 percent; unemployment: 2.8 percent

1975   Creation of CII-Honeywell-Bull to promote a national computer industry

Social transfer payments as a percent of GDP: 23.8 percent

Annual inflation: 11.8 percent; unemployment: 4.1 percent

1976   First commercial flight of Concorde

Raymond Barre becomes prime minister and minister of finance

Parisian garbage collectors strike for two weeks

Raymond Barre announces his anti-inflation plan which includes price freezes, wage controls, credit restrictions, tax increases for individuals and companies, as well as on gasoline and alcohol, and investment and export incentives

Twelve new nuclear reactors planned

Employees laid off for economic reasons guaranteed 90 percent salary

Annual inflation: 9.6 percent; unemployment: 4.4 percent

1977   Unemployment exceeds 1 million for the first time

A new Barre government formed

Crisis in the steel industry; negotiations over employment reductions begin amid massive strikes

Second phase of Barre Plan: decontrolling of prices and lowering of value added tax; industry-wide collective bargaining agreements signed to moderate prices increases

Law passed requiring companies to make an annual report on employment relations in their company (*bilan social de l'entreprise*)

Jacques Chirac elected mayor of Paris

New measures to prevent youth unemployment enacted

National multi-industry agreement on early retirement at age sixty enacted

Left political parties break off negotiations for an electoral campaign under their Common Program

Concorde receives authorization for Paris–New York flights

Annual inflation: 9.4 percent; unemployment: 4.9 percent

1978   Gaullist-conservative victory in parliamentary elections

Third Barre government formed

Some industrial prices decontrolled

Price of bread freed for the first time in decades

Peugeot-Citröen-Chrysler enter into an agreement

Annual inflation: 9.1 percent; unemployment: 5.2 percent

1979   European Monetary System (EMS) created; eight EEC nations agree to control currency fluctuations; the central banks intervene in order to defend their currencies' parity

The ECU (European Currency Unit) becomes the EEC's official currency

British Aerospace, Belgium, and Spain join the Airbus Industrie consortium

Renault buys American Motors Company

Annual inflation: 10.8 percent; unemployment: 5.9 percent

1980   Matra, an electronics company, takes control of Hachette, a publishing house

Social transfer payments as a percent of GDP: 27 percent

Annual inflation: 13.6 percent; unemployment: 6.3 percent

1981   Greece enters the EEC

François Mitterrand becomes president, dissolves the National Assembly

Socialist landslide in parliamentary elections: Pierre Mauroy becomes prime minister; his government includes four Communist ministers

Social programs enacted: minimum wage increased 10 percent; 54,000 public sector jobs created;

Four billion francs made available to companies for job-creating and export-stimulation activities

27.6 percent in public expenditures voted for 1982 budget

Nationalizations: a law to nationalize five industrial groups: CGE (Compagnie Générale d'Electricité), Pechiney-Ugine-Kuhlman, Saint-Gobain-Pont-à-Mousson, Rhône-Poulenc, and Thomson-Brandt; the conversion of the debt of the two leading steel companies Usinor and Sacilor into state holdings; and a 51 percent state holding in Matra and Dassault; nationalizing the main banks and the two leading investment-bank holding companies, Suez and Paribas

Thirty nuclear plants in operation

Annual inflation: 13.4 percent; unemployment: 7.4 percent

1982   Socialist social legislation enacted: fifth week paid vacation; a thirty-nine-hour week with no reduction of salary; retirement at sixty (fifty-seven for the public sector)

Pierre Bérégovoy becomes minister of solidarity and social affairs

Wage and price controls enacted

Collective bargaining agreements signed to moderate wages and price increases; indexing wages and prices ended

Four Auroux Laws are voted to reinforce the Labor Code: by providing new channels for direct worker expression in working conditions and organization; by reinforcing the role of worker representatives inside companies; by requiring employers and unions to bargain collectively; and by establishing committees on health, safety and working conditions

Law granting more power to local governments enacted

State radio monopoly ended

Annual inflation: 11.8 percent; unemployment: 8.1 percent

1983   The Left suffers an electoral loss in municipal elections

New Mauroy government formed: Jacques Delors becomes minister of economy and finances; Laurent Fabius minister of industry

New austerity program—1 percent surtax and "loan" of 10 percent of taxable income; taxes on cigarettes and alcohol are raised; exchange controls tightened; public firms asked to cut deficits; the franc is devaluated for the third time since 1981

European Spacelab sent into orbit aboard Columbia

Annual inflation: 9.6 percent; unemployment: 8.3 percent

1984   Major industrial restructuring plan including the introduction of up to two years' paid "conversion leave" for workers facing redundancies in the steel, coal, and shipbuilding industries; and the creation of up to twelve special "conversion zones," in which the development of new firms will be encouraged through tax advantages

First private cable television station created

Prime Minister Mauroy resigns, replaced by Laurent Fabius: his goal is to help companies become more competitive

Administrative formalities for creating new companies simplified

More than 2.5 million people out of work

Government decontrols prices; wage increases to be held to 4.5 percent

Forty-one nuclear plants in operation; France is the second largest producer of nuclear power in world after the United States

Annual inflation: 7.4 percent; unemployment: 9.7 percent;

1985   Georges Besse is appointed CEO of Renault

Annual inflation: 5.8 percent; unemployment: 10.1 percent

1986   Spain and Portugal enter the EEC

Conservative victory in the parliamentary elections, beginning the "cohabitation" of the Socialist president Mitterrand and a conservative prime minister Jacques Chirac

Privatization announced for nationalized companies including Havas, Elf-Aquitaine, the banks and insurance companies nationalized in 1945, and the banks and companies nationalized in 1982

State requirements for authorization of layoffs eased

Employers exempted from paying social security contributions for employees between ages of sixteen and twenty-five

New CEOs appointed for twelve of the twenty-five most important nationalized companies

Privatization law is voted on by the National Assembly and the Senate

Rules easing the restrictions on part-time, temporary, and seasonal employment enacted

Fifteen new CEOs are appointed to head the nationalized banks; they are mainly professionals close to the right-wing parties

Privatization: the state sells 11 percent (out of 66.8 percent) of its shares of Elf-Aquitaine

Adoption of two new decrees encouraging employees' financial participation in their companies and employee participation in management

Agreement on redundancy procedures signed by CNPF (employers' union) and CFDT, CFTC, and FO (trade unions); CGT and CGC refuse to sign

Cabinet approves two bills for the final reform easing layoff procedures

Georges Besse, CEO of Renault, is murdered by terrorists; he is replaced by Raymond Lévy

Saint-Gobain is successfully privatized: 1,547,000 individual shareholders buy 50 percent of the capital

Student strikes protest state proposal to introduce tuition and selection requirements

Wildcat strikes at the railways and the electricity company (December 1986–January 1987)

Annual unemployment: 10.3 percent; inflation: 2.1 percent

1987   Television station TF 1 privatized

Management granted greater flexibility in setting work hours

First employee profit-sharing agreement in a public enterprise is signed at EDF-GDF (electricity and gas) by four union confederations: CFDT, FO, CGC, and CFTC (The Communist CGT refuses to sign.)

Annual unemployment: 10.0 percent; inflation: 2.0 percent

1988   Mitterrand elected president for a second seven-year term; Michel Rocard named prime minister, heading a Socialist-Centrist government.

1992   Single Market: ending of all trade barriers among Common Market countries.

Appendix II

Glossary of Terms

agrégés—The title given to those who have successfully passed the *agrégation*, a highly competitive exam or *concours*, enabling them to obtain a tenured position as a high school teacher or university professor.

Airbus—Manufacturer of commerical airplanes, a joint venture between France, West Germany, Great Britain, and Spain.

Ariane—The European rocket successfully launched in 1983. Originally financed by the European Space Agency and now produced by Arianespace, a private company with backers in eleven European countries, more than 50 percent in France.

Barre—Raymond Barre, prime minister from 1976–81 under Giscard; UDF candidate for the presidency in 1988.

Bourse—Stock exchange, usually refers to the Paris stock exchange, especially when spelled with a capital letter.

Bouygues—Francis Bouygues, founder and CEO of the construction company bearing his name, the leader in France and in the world; also, the owner of the first privatized TV channel in France, TF1.

BSN—The largest food company in France; tenth largest in the Common Market.

Bull—French computer company. Originally independent, Bull became a subsidiary of General Electric, and then of Honeywell before being nationalized in 1982. On the list of companies to be privatized, Bull is the largest shareholder of Honeywell-Bull, Inc., Honeywell's former American computer division.

Chirac—Jacques Chirac, chosen prime minister of France in March 1986 by François Mitterrand to participate in the cohabitation of the 1986–88 period. Also, presidential candidate of the rightist RPR (Rassemblement pour la république) in 1988.

CGE—Compagnie Générale d'Electricité, one of five large industrial corporations nationalized in France in 1981–82 and on the list of companies to be privatized by the Chirac government.

classes préparatoires—One- or two-year academic programs between high school and higher education that prepare students to take the competitive entrance exams for the prestigious grandes écoles.

CNCL—Commission Nationale de la Communication et des Libertés: a commission set up to oversee all audiovisual activities in France. Explained in detail by Pierre Barret.

CLT—Compagnie luxembourgeoise de télédiffusion, parent company of Radio-Télé-Luxembourg.

Code du Travail—The French name for the body of labor laws that govern employees' rights.

COGEMA—Compagnie générale des matières nucléaires, French uranium producing company totally owned by the French Atomic Energy Commission (Commissariat à l'énergie atomique).

cohabitation—The situation that exists when the president of France is of a different political party from the dominant party in government, the majority party in the Assemblée Nationale, from which the prime minister and cabinet are normally chosen. Cohabitation occurred for the first time in the Fifth Republic from 1986 to 1988, when the Socialist president François Mitterrand chose the rightist Jacques Chirac as prime minister.

Colbert Committee—Founded in 1954 by Jean Guerlain, the "Comité Colbert" is made up of seventy French manufacturers of luxury goods. The aim of this committee is to transmit a cultural message representing a certain image of France.

collectivitiés—The word used by the French to refer to units of local government.

comité d'entreprise—A committee consisting of employee representatives, elected by all employees. These committees, required by law in companies having fifty employees or more, have three functions: to advise employees of company policy, to manage the company's budget for social activities, and to give employees the opportunity to express their opinion with regard to company policy. The management is obliged to listen to this opinion, but is not obliged to heed it.

Comité Image de la France—A committee created by the Ministry of Industry to study the image of France; dissolved upon submission of its report in July 1985.

Commission des Operations de Bourse—Known as the C.O.B.; created in 1968 to oversee the Paris and provincial stock markets, to regulate operations, and protect investors.

compensatory payments—Under the Common Market's common agricultural policy, the amount added to the price of agricultural products that are transferred across borders to compensate farmers for the effects of exchange rate fluctuations.

Confédération Général du Travail—A French trade union affiliated with the Communist party. The largest union; it has had declining membership in recent years.

Confédération Française Démocratique du Travail—The second largest union in France, not affiliated with any political party, but with Socialist tendencies.

Conseil National du Patronat Français—The major association of French employers (*patrons*); serves as the voice and negotiating agent of owners and management with unions. Considered as an owners "union" in France where "union" is defined as an association of persons in the same profession or in the same sector, with the purpose of defending their collective interests.

Conseil constitutionnel—An independent body that decides if laws are in accord with the Constitution of the Fifth Republic.

Crédit National—Bank created by the government that manages government borrowing and makes loans to business and industry.

De Benedetti—Carlo De Benedetti, the chairman of Olivetti, who is investing heavily in Europe.

decentralization movement—Decentralization began in France in the 1960s with the government's realization of the negative economic and political effects of having a country in which all decisions are made in the capital. France was officially divided into twenty-two regions in 1973 and given local regional governments in 1981.

Le Défi américain—A book written by Jean-Jacques Servan-Schreiber in 1967. Translated as *The American Challenge*, it criticized the French for their backward management style and exhorted them to copy the Americans.

délégué du personnel—Elected by the employees in companies having ten or more employees, the délégué du personnel is the intermediary between the management and the workers or employees for all complaints or demands, individual or collective.

dirigisme—The term used to connote the French tradition of state intervention in society and the economy.

Ecole Normale Supérieure—A *grande école* founded in 1794 to create professors and scientists. "Normale Sup," as it is called familiarly, counts many well-known French people among its graduates, including Jean-Paul Sartre and Georges Pompidou.

EEC—The European Economic Community, also known as the Common Market, includes twelve West European countries: Belgium, Denmark, France, Great Britain, Greece, Ireland, Italy, Luxembourg, The Netherlands, Portugal, Spain, and West Germany.

EMS—European monetary system; an agreement (1979) among the Common Market countries according to which they stabilize their currencies through the use of the "ecu," or European currency unit.

ENA—Acronym for the Ecole Nationale d'Administration, created in 1945 to form the highest level of civil servants.

ESSEC—Ecole Supérieure des sciences économiques et commerciales, a leading business school.

Eurodollar, eurofranc—A dollar deposited in a non-American bank in Europe by Europeans or Americans; a franc deposited in a non-French bank outside France, but in Europe.

L'Express—A weekly newsmagazine in France, somewhat like *Time* or *Newsweek*.

Fabius—Laurent Fabius, a Socialist, was prime minister of France from 1983 to 1986.

Force Ouvrière—Moderate trade union in France, with Socialist tendencies but no party affiliation.

GATT—General Agreement on Tariffs and Trade, a multilateral trade agreement established in 1948 among ninety countries, mostly developing nations.

Giscard d'Estaing—Valéry Giscard d'Estaing, president of France from 1973 to 1981, is the leader of the rightist political party, the UDF (Union Démocratique des Français).

Golden Share—Shares involving special privileges.

Goldsmith Group—Group of companies owned by Jimmy Goldsmith, British-French businessman, former owner of *L'Express*, considered to be the third wealthiest person in France.

grande école—Equivalent in prestige to American Ivy League colleges, the French *grandes écoles* are not open to all students with the *baccalauréat* as is true of the French University. To be admitted to a *grande école*, students must take a grueling two-year preparatory course and then pass a highly selective exam. A diploma from the most prestigious *grandes écoles* (Polytechnique, Normale Sup, HEC, ENA) assures a successful career to a much greater extent than a similar diploma in the United States.

Hachette Group—The largest publisher of books, newspapers, and periodicals in France.

Havas—Founded in the 1830s as a news agency, Havas is now a semipublic company with activities in the advertising and communications sectors.

HEC—Acronym for the Ecole des Hautes études commerciales, a leading *grande école* for business in France.

Hersant Group—Publisher controlling more than 25 percent of regional dailies and almost 40 percent of national daily newspapers in France, in addition to a number of specialized magazines; is also part owner of the new private television channel 5.

hexagonal—France is familiarly referred to as the "Hexagon"; the adjective hexagonal, therefore, refers to something that is completely French, without consideration of the outside world.

IDI—Institut de développement industriel, a quasi-public organization created in 1970 to advise and financially aid businesses considered to be of national interest, especially in the area of restructuring of industry.

INA—Institut National de la Communication Audiovisuelle, an agency that supervises radio and television archives.

INSEE—Institut National de la Statistique et des Etudes économiques, the government agency responsible for collecting and collating statistics about France.

Institut d'études politiques (de Paris)—Called "Sciences-Po"; the *grande école* for the study of economics and political science.

ISA—Institut supérieure des affaires, a business graduate school associated with HEC that offers a program leading to the equivalent of an American MBA.

Lagardère—Jean-Luc Lagardère, CEO of Matra-Hachette in 1987 during Hachette's attempts to acquire one of the newly privatized television channels.

lame duck—A company experiencing financial difficulties over an extended period of time; known in France as a *canard boiteux*.

Jack Lang—The minister of culture from 1981 to 1986.

John Law—In 1716 John Law, a Scot, created a bank in which he convinced people to buy stock. A success until 1719, the bank failed in 1720 because of oversubscription. This is often cited as the cause for the traditional French suspicion of the stock market and consequent reticence to invest in business.

LMBO's—Leveraged management buyouts.

Lomé agreements—Trade agreements (the first in 1975, the second in 1979) according to which the Common Market offers preferential treatment and aid to developing nations in Africa, the Caribbean, and the South Pacific.

Maghreb—The term used in France to refer to the former North African colonies of Algeria, Morocco, and Tunisia.

marché unique—Refers to the lifting of trade barriers among the Common Market countries in 1992, resulting in the creation of a unified or "single" market in Europe.

Marianne—Allegorical figure for the French Republic; a woman with a phrygian bonnet (symbol of the French Revolution); busts of Marianne began to appear in France in the 1870s, first modeled after a statue, and more recently after Brigitte Bardot and Catherine Deneuve.

Matra—French high tech and arms producer, partially nationalized in 1982.

Mitterrand—François Mitterrand, leader of the Socialist party, elected president of France in 1981 and 1988.

National Assembly—The French legislative body, equivalent to the American House of Representatives, consisting of 577 members (called *députés*) elected by universal suffrage for a term of five years. The other branch of the French parliament, the Senate, is made up of 319 senators elected by indirect suffrage for a term of nine years.

nationalization—The procedure whereby the state assumes ownership of previously private enterprises. There have been three periods of nationalization in France: in 1936–37 under the Popular Front; in 1946–47 after the Second World War in order to speed up the industrial reconstruction of the country and punish industrialists who had collaborated with the occupation forces; and in 1981–82 when the Socialist government nationalized all French banks and five major corporations.

1992—In 1992, the Common Market countries will abolish all trade barriers among themselves and establish a completely free trade zone.

OECD—Organization for Economic Cooperation and Development, created in 1960 and now having twenty-four members who try to coordinate their economic and social policy to promote their own economic well being and to cooperate in efforts to help developing nations.

PC—Parti communiste; the Communist party in France, also referred to as the PCF.

plan—France adopted economic planning in 1946. There have been eight plans since then, the last of which, proposed for the period 1981–85, was never approved by the French parliament (National Assembly and Senate). The French plans are intended as guidelines to orient economic development and are not rigid programs as in the Eastern block nations.

Polytechnique—The most prestigious of the *grandes écoles* (familiarly known in France as "X"); founded in 1794 for the purpose of giving a scientific formation to future military officers and high-ranking civil servants.

privatization—The procedure by which companies previously owned by the state are returned to the private sector. Privatization was begun by the Chirac government in 1986.

PS—Parti socialiste; the Socialist party in France.

Rocard—Michel Rocard, one of the leaders of the Socialist party in France, a member of the cabinet between 1981 and 1986, and a candidate for the presidency in 1988; named prime minister in June 1988.

RPR—Rassemblement pour la République, a rightist party in France, led by Jacques Chirac, known in English as the Rally for the Republic.

Russian loans—From 1888 to 1917 more than 1 million French invested in the "Russian loans" that became worthless in 1917. This experience is cited, along with John Law's bank in the eighteenth century, as a cause of the traditional French reticence to invest in the stock market.

Schlumberger—French conglomerate especially present in the oil drilling equipment field.

Second market—A new stock market created in France in 1983, the *second marché* allowed smaller companies to go public by decreasing initial costs and by lowering the requirement of stock offered to 10 percent of capital.

Société Générale de Belgique—A Belgian banking company.

le système D—The approach adopted by the French to overcome the difficulties and constraints resulting from overregulation and overwhelming bureaucracy. "D" stands for *débrouillard*, someone who can find a way out of any difficult situation.

SNCF—Acronym for the French railroads or *Société Nationale des Chemins de Fer*.

SNECMA—Société nationale d'étude et de construction de moteurs d'aviation: a company 90 percent-owned by the state.

SOFIRAD—Public company that manages government investment in the peripheral radio stations in France, among which are Radio Monte-Carlo and Sud-Radio.

Sofres-Le Point—French opinion survey organization.

Supaéro—Ecole supérieure d'aéronautique, *grande école* for aeronautical engineering.

Tapie—Bernard Tapie, a French entrepreneur who has become famous by buying up bankrupt firms at low prices and turning them around. A hero to most young people, he is scorned by the business establishment.

TDF—Télédiffusion de France, a public company in charge of transmission for television channels and radio stations in France.

Télématique—French term for the integration of telecommunications and computers.

TGV—Acronym for the French high-speed train or *train à grande vitesse*.

UDF—Union Démocratique Française, the center-right party of the former president, Valéry Giscard d'Estaing. Represented in the 1988 presidential elections by Raymond Barre.

Union de la gauche—Alliance of the left-wing parties—Socialist, Communist and radicals—which supported a common program from 1972 to 1980.

Valéry—Paul Valéry, well-known French poet, 1871–1945.

Simone Veil—Minister of Health from 1974 to 1978 during the presidency of Valéry Giscard d'Estaing, and president of the European Parliament (legislative branch of the Common Market) from 1982 to 1984, Simone Veil is one of the best known and most respected women in French politics.

zone franc—Group of countries whose currencies are tied to the French franc. *La zone franc* includes France, its overseas territories, and a number of African countries.

Index

Editors and Contributors

JEAN-PAUL ANGÉ is vice-president of Global Securities, a subsidiary of Crédit Lyonnais in New York. He was previously the director of the French Industrial Development Agency, responsible for the DATAR's three U.S. offices in New York, Chicago, and Los Angeles. Mr. Angé, a graduate of the Ecole Polytechnique, has served at the French Ministry of Defense.

PIERRE BARRET, communications consultant and vice-president of SETTE, publisher of specialty journals, was president of Europe I, a major French radio station, from 1981 to 1986. Previously associated with both *L'Express* and *Le Point*, Mr. Barret has coauthored a series of historical novels based on the Crusades and written articles on medieval and nineteenth-century French history. He is a graduate of HEC.

JEAN-PIERRE BEAUDOIN, a public relations consultant, is managing director of Information et Entreprise in Paris, and also chairman of the French Public Relations Consultants Association. Director of the public relations department at the University of Paris IV (Sorbonne) since 1982, Mr. Beaudoin is a chevalier in the Ordre des Palmes Académiques.

SERGE BELLANGER is executive vice-president and general manager of CIC-Union Européenne, International et Cie., and the U.S. general representative of the CIC Group. He is also national president of the French-American Chamber of Commerce in the United States. Mr. Bellanger is a member of the editorial board of *The World of Banking* and a columnist for *The Bankers' Magazine*. He is a chevalier of the Légion d'Honneur.

OLIVIER BLANCHARD is professor of economics at the Massachusetts Institute of Technology. He has been a visiting professor at the University of Paris and Columbia University. He has written articles for many economic journals, contributed chapters on various economic topics, and coauthored *Lectures on Macroeconomics*.

JEAN BOISSONNAT is editor-in-chief of the Expansion Press Group, publisher of *L'Expansion*, *La Lettre de l'Expansion*, *L'Entreprise*, and *La Tribune de l'Economie*. From 1975 to 1986 he was a business journalist with a regular program on Europe I, a French radio station. Author of *La Politique des Revenues* and *Journal de Crise*, his latest book is entitled *Crise, krach, boom*. A graduate of the Institut d'études politiques de Paris, he taught there from 1966 to 1971.

LYDIE BONNET, a research associate at the Harvard Business School, was previously marketing director of Malesherbe-Publications in France. She was on the staff of the French Ministry of Culture, and holds degrees from the Institut d'études politiques de Paris and from HEC-JF (Ecole des Huates Etudes Commerciales Jeunes Filles).

JEAN-FRANÇOIS CARRERAS is a partner in the international law firm, Coudert Brothers. A graduate of the University of Paris law school, he also holds a diploma from the Institut d'études politiques de Paris.

BEATRICE DAUTRESME is vice-president, general manager of L'Oréal Cosmetics, a division of Cosmair, the U.S. licensee of L'Oréal. A graduate of the Institut national des langues et civilisations orientales in Paris. Ms. Dautresme worked as an international translator before deciding on a career in business.

ANDRÉ DOUCET, currently director of acquisitions and new business development for the Gillette Company in France, was president of their former subsidiary, S. T. Dupont, from 1976 to 1986. He was president of the Colbert Committee and has been a permanent member of the French Commercial Science Academy since 1974.

BRUNO DUFOUR is president of the Ecole Supérieure de Commerce de Lyon, of which he was dean from 1982 until 1987. A graduate of ESSEC, he also has a master's degree in economic psychology and has studied in the United States. He is general manager of a group of small textile companies in the Lyon area.

JUDITH FROMMER is Senior Preceptor in Romance Languages and Literatures at Harvard University. She has organized several conferences on French business at Harvard and is the originator of the French for Business course.

DANIEL JOUVE, currently managing partner of his own executive search firm—

Jouve, Esnault, et Associés—was general manager of Russell Reynolds France from 1978 to 1986. Previously director of the *Nouvel Economiste*, he has authored *Votre carrière, comment la piloter* and, more recently, *Capitaines d'entreprise*. He received an MBA from the Harvard Business School in 1963.

JEAN-PAUL LARÇON has been dean of HEC since 1982. Prior to that he was dean and professor of strategic planning at C.E.R.A.M., the business school in the technical park, Sophia-Antipolis, near Nice. He has coauthored a number of books, the latest of which is *Structures de Pouvoir et Identité de l'Entreprise*, and has written numerous articles on management.

CLAUDE LEGAL has been the commercial counselor (Conseiller commercial) and director of the Trade Relations Office of the French Embassy in New York since 1984. He has served in various capacities related to trade in the French foreign service in South America, Europe, and Africa. A graduate of both HEC and ENA, Mr. LeGal was a professor at the Ecole Supérieure de Commerce de Rouen from 1980 to 1984 and during that period also lectured at HEC, ENA, and ESSEC.

JEAN LÉVY is general manager, (Administrateur Général) of Chaussures André in France. From 1969 until 1987, he held many positions with L'Oréal-France, the last of which was president-chief executive officer of Cosmair, Inc., U.S. licensee of L'Oréal. Mr. Lévy has a diploma from the Institut d'études politiques de Paris and attended graduate school at Yale University.

YVES-FRÉDÉRIC LIVIAN is professor of management at the Ecole Supérieure de Commerce de Lyon and has taught at the Université de Lyon II et III. He has been a visiting professor at the Pace University Business School in New York, and has written numerous articles on organizational problems and industrial relations. He is a graduate of the Institut d'études politiques de Paris and holds a doctorate in industrial relations.

JEAN LOYRETTE is a founding member and senior partner of the law firm Gide Loyrette Nouel. His book, *Dénationaliser*, describes the advantages, problems, and processes of denationalization. He has written numerous articles and given many lectures on a variety of legal topics. A graduate of the Insitut d'études politiques de Paris, he studied law at the University of Paris and received a Doctor of Letters from Oxford University.

JANICE McCORMICK is Associate Professor of Organizational Behavior and Human Resources Management in the Graduate School of Business Administration at Harvard University. She has written extensively on French business and political economy.

JACQUES MAISONROUGE is the former president and chairman of the board of the IBM World Trade Corporation. Director general in the French Ministry of Industry from 1986 to 1987, he has been president of the Centre Français du Commerce Extérieur (French Foreign Trade Board) since January 1, 1988. A graduate engineer of the Ecole Centrale de Paris, Mr. Maisonrouge has been active in promoting the image of France in the United States.

CLAUDE MARCUS has spent his entire career at Publicis, a leading French advertising agency. Since 1984 he has been president of Publicis International, a network of twenty-four agencies in twelve countries. He is president of the Advertising Consumer Commission in France. A member of the Commission Nationale de la Consommation, he is a chevalier of the Légion d'Honneur, and holds diplomas in economics and law from the University of Paris.

JEAN-DANIEL TORDJMAN has been minister for economic and commercial affairs at the French embassy in the United States since 1985. He has also served as deputy secretary in the Ministry of Commerce, Small Business and Tourism, and as special counselor for international affairs to the Minister of Research and Technology. He is a graduate of the Ecole Nationale d'Administration.

JEAN-LOUIS VILGRAIN is president and chairman of the board of the Grands Moulins de Paris in France and chairman of the Vie de France Corporation in the United States. He is president of the European Foundation for the Economy and the National Committee of Industrial Mills in France. He is a member of the advisory board of the International Finance Corporation in Washington, and has received many decorations, among which is chevalier of the Légion d'Honneur.